God's Wisdom
—for—
Daily Living

God's Wisdom
—for—
Daily Living

from the
New King James Version

Every verse in Proverbs topically arranged

Thomas Nelson Publishers
Nashville

Scripture quotations are from the NEW KING JAMES VER-
SION. Copyright © 1979, 1980, 1982, Thomas Nelson Inc.,
Publishers

Copyright © 1984 by Thomas Nelson Inc.

Published in Nashville, Tennessee, by Thomas Nelson, Inc.,
and distributed in Canada by Lawson Falle, Ltd., Cam-
bridge, Ontario.

Printed in the United States of America.

ISBN 0-8407-6753-6   CB

ISBN 0-8407-3155-8   PB

The fear of the LORD
is the beginning of wisdom.

Proverbs 9:10

CONTENTS

Introduction

And God gave Solomon wisdom and
exceedingly great understanding, and
largeness of heart like the sand on the
seashore. Thus Solomon's wisdom ex-
celled the wisdom of all the men of the
East and all the wisdom of Egypt. For
he was wiser than all men—than Ethan
the Ezrahite, and Heman, Chalcol, and
Darda, the sons of Mahol; and his fame
was in all the surrounding nations. He
spoke three thousand proverbs, and his
songs were one thousand and five. Also
he spoke of trees, from the cedar tree of
Lebanon even to the hyssop that springs
out of the wall; he spoke also of animals, of birds, of creeping things, and
of fish. And men of all nations, from
all the kings of the earth who had
heard of his wisdom, came to hear the
wisdom of Solomon (1 Kings 4:29–34).

Of the three thousand proverbs spoken by
Solomon, less than a third have been preserved
in the Scripture. The book of Proverbs consists
of several collections of proverbs written by
Solomon and other ancient wise men. Chapters
one through nine contain a collection of wisdom discourses, each written about a moral
theme. A few short discourses are found

elsewhere in the book, such as the poem on the virtuous wife (see 31:10–31), but the majority of the book contains a collection of independent proverbs written on various topics arranged in random order.

The proverbs were written in Hebrew poetry. The individual proverbs are unique poetic units of two or more lines. Each is complete in itself, expressing one key thought. Frequently the thought is expressed in its positive sense in one poetic line, and in its negative sense in the other line.

The choice of words, combined with poetic rhythm and parallelism, produced pithy sayings on moral themes that make permanent impressions on the minds of men. Because each proverb is complete in itself, it stands alone without need for context or supporting argument.

Apart from those chapters that contain wisdom discourses, the proverbs are not arranged by topic but have random order. This may have been intentional to provide each chapter with wise thoughts on a variety of topics. Although it is not convenient for a topical study of the proverbs, the arrangement is beneficial for regular reading. The present work arranges the proverbs for convenient topical study and devotional reading. It is not presented as an improvement over the biblical order, but as a study aid.

A topical study of Solomon's proverbs reveals that God was at the center of all his thoughts.

The proverbs contrast two opposing ways of life, the way of wisdom and the way of folly.

The wise person has a wholesome relationship with God and men; he knows how to manage his life, and he has good personal characteristics. He has excellent relationships with spouse and children, with friends and society; he works hard and prospers. He readily receives instruction, seeks guidance from God and wise counselors, and plans his life for the mutual benefit of all. He is emotionally well adjusted, is motivated by godly love, and has a good share of righteous characteristics such as faithfulness, truthfulness, sound speech, humility, self-control, justice, and moral strength. He has a vibrant meaningful life and a sure hope for the hereafter.

The fool is the opposite of the wise person; he follows the ways of folly, is known for excessive wrath and wine, and usually ends in poverty and destruction.

Both wise person and fool receive recompense from God. The wise person is rewarded for righteousness and the fool punished for folly. The wise are advised to practice sincere worship in the fear of the Lord; fools are warned that mere ritual is an offense to the God of holiness.

The proverbs are arranged under thirty-one topics for the convenience of daily devotional reading. Within each topic, the proverbs are arranged in logical order to follow a theme. Paragraph headings are provided to mark the progress of thought. It is the hope of the author and publisher that this topical arrangement of the proverbs will be of blessing and benefit to all.

=== 1 ===

The Great God Who Formed All Things

There is no wisdom or understanding
Or counsel against the LORD (21:30).

Solomon's theology is not declared in formal statements. It is revealed indirectly in his teachings on other topics. God is the center of all his thoughts; He is the focal point of all his proverbs. Solomon knew God as the all-powerful creator. Being everywhere and knowing everything, God is the sovereign ruler of His universe. Although He remains ever mysterious, His righteous and holy character is manifested by the justice of His dealings; and His infinite love is expressed by His mercy and grace. His person is revealed through His Son who has descended from heaven and ascended into heaven. His precepts are expounded in His divinely inspired Word, which is perfect in purpose, purity, and practice. The great God who formed all things is worthy of all worship and praise.

God Is All-Powerful Creator

The LORD by wisdom founded the earth;
By understanding He established the heavens;
By His knowledge the depths were broken up,
And clouds drop down the dew (3:19–20).

The hearing ear and the seeing eye,
The LORD has made both of them (20:12).

The rich and the poor have this in common,
The LORD is the maker of them all (22:2).

There are three things which are too wonderful
    for me,
Yes, four which I do not understand:
The way of an eagle in the air,
The way of a serpent on a rock,
The way of a ship in the midst of the sea,
And the way of a man with a virgin (30:18–19).

There are three things which are majestic in
    pace,
Yes, four which are stately in walk:
A lion, which is mighty among beasts
And does not turn away from any;
A greyhound,
A male goat also,
And a king whose troops are with him
    (30:29–31).

God Is Everywhere

The eyes of the LORD are in every place,
Keeping watch on the evil and the good (15:3).

God Knows Everything

For the ways of man are before the eyes of the
   LORD,
And He ponders all his paths (5:21).

Hell and Destruction are before the LORD
So how much more the hearts of the sons of
   men (15:11).

There is no wisdom or understanding
Or counsel against the LORD (21:30).

God Is Sovereign

The king's heart is in the hand of the LORD
Like the rivers of water;
He turns it wherever He wishes (21:1).

The LORD has made all things for Himself,
Yes, even the wicked for the day of doom
   (16:4).

God Is Holy

Those who are of a perverse heart are an
   abomination to the LORD,
But such as are blameless in their ways are His
   delight (11:20).

For the perverse person is an abomination to the
   LORD,
But His secret counsel is with the upright (3:32).

These six things the LORD hates,
Yes, seven are an abomination to Him:
A proud look,
A lying tongue,
Hands that shed innocent blood,
A heart that devises wicked plans,
Feet that are swift in running to evil,
A false witness who speaks lies,
And one who sows discord among brethren
  (6:16–19).

Everyone who is proud in heart is an
  abomination to the LORD,
Though they join forces, none will go
  unpunished (16:5).

Lying lips are an abomination to the LORD
But those who deal truthfully are His delight
  (12:22).

Diverse weights are an abomination to the
  LORD,
And a false balance is not good (20:23).

A false balance is an abomination to the LORD,
But a just weight is His delight (11:1).

Diverse weights and diverse measures,
They are both alike, an abomination to the
  LORD (20:10).

The sacrifice of the wicked is an abomination to
  the LORD,
But the prayer of the upright is His delight
  (15:8).

The sacrifice of the wicked is an abomination;
How much more when he brings it with wicked
   intent! (21:27).

The way of the wicked is an abomination to the
   LORD,
But He loves him who follows righteousness
   (15:9).

The thoughts of the wicked are an abomination
   to the LORD,
But the words of the pure are pleasant (15:26).

One who turns away his ear from hearing the
   law,
Even his prayer shall be an abomination (28:9).

He who justifies the wicked, and he who
   condemns the just,
Both of them alike are an abomination to the
   LORD (17:15).

God Is Just

Do not envy the oppressor,
And choose none of his ways;
For the perverse person is an abomination to the
   LORD,
But His secret counsel is with the upright.
The curse of the LORD is on the house of the
   wicked,
But He blesses the habitation of the just.
Surely He scorns the scornful,
But gives grace to the humble.

The wise shall inherit glory,
But shame shall be the legacy of fools
    (3:31–35).

For the ways of man are before the eyes of the
    LORD,
And He ponders all his paths.
His own iniquities entrap the wicked man,
And he is caught in the cords of his sin.
He shall die for lack of instruction,
And in the greatness of his folly he shall go
    astray (5:21–23).

A just weight and balance are the LORD'S;
All the weights in the bag are His work (16:11).

Every way of a man is right in his own eyes,
But the LORD weighs the hearts (21:2).

The righteous God wisely considers the house
    of the wicked,
Overthrowing the wicked for their wickedness
    (21:12).

Do not rob the poor because he is poor,
Nor oppress the afflicted at the gate;
For the LORD will plead their cause,
And plunder the soul of those who plunder
    them (22:22–23).

Do not remove the ancient landmark,
Nor enter the fields of the fatherless;
For their Redeemer is mighty;
He will plead their cause against you
    (23:10–11).

Deliver those who are drawn toward death,
And hold back those stumbling to the slaughter.
If you say, "Surely we did not know this,"
Does not He who weighs the hearts consider it?
He who keeps your soul, does He not know it?
And will He not render to each man according
   to his deeds? (24:11–12).

Do not rejoice when your enemy falls,
And do not let your heart be glad when he
   stumbles;
Lest the LORD see it, and it displease Him,
And He turn away His wrath from him
   (24:17–18).

Many seek the ruler's favor,
But justice for man comes from the LORD
   (29:26).

God Is Gracious

The poor man and the oppressor have this in
   common:
The LORD gives light to the eyes of both (29:13).

God Is Merciful

The great God who formed all things gives the
   fool his hire and the transgressor his wages
   (26:10).

The horse is prepared for the day of battle,
But deliverance is of the LORD (21:31).

God Is Mysterious

It is the glory of God to conceal a matter,
But the glory of kings is to search out a matter
  (25:2).

God Has a Son

Who has ascended into heaven, or descended?
Who has gathered the wind in His fists?
Who has bound the waters in a garment?
Who has established all the ends of the earth?
What is His name, and what is His Son's name,
If you know? (30:4)

God's Word Is Perfect

Perfect in Purpose

To know wisdom and instruction,
To perceive the words of understanding,
To receive the instruction of wisdom,
Justice, judgment, and equity;
To give prudence to the simple,
To the young man knowledge and discretion—
A wise man will hear and increase learning,
And a man of understanding will attain wise
  counsel,
To understand a proverb and an enigma,
The words of the wise and their riddles (1:2–6).

Perfect in Purity

Every word of God is pure;
He is a shield to those who put their trust in
  Him.

Do not add to His words,
Lest He reprove you, and you be found a liar
  (30:5–6).

Perfect in Practice
He who despises the word will be destroyed,
But he who fears the commandment will be
  rewarded.
The law of the wise is a fountain of life,
To turn one away from the snares of death
  (13:13–14).

He who keeps the commandment keeps his soul,
But he who is careless of his ways will die
  (19:16).

He who heeds the word wisely will find good,
And whoever trusts in the LORD, happy is he
  (16:20).

Where there is no revelation, the people cast off
  restraint;
But happy is he who keeps the law (29:18).

Those who forsake the law praise the wicked,
But such as keep the law contend with them
  (28:4).

Have I not written to you excellent things
Of counsels and knowledge,
That I may make you know the certainty of the
  words of truth,
That you may answer words of truth
To those who send to you? (22:20–21).

=== 2 ===

Wisdom Is Primary

Get wisdom! Get understanding!
Do not forget, nor turn away from the
  words of my mouth.
Do not forsake her, and she will preserve
  you;
Love her, and she will keep you.
Wisdom is the principal thing;
Therefore get wisdom.
And in all your getting,
  get understanding.
Exalt her, and she will promote you;
She will bring you honor, when you em-
  brace her.
She will place on your head an ornament
  of grace;
A crown of glory she will deliver to you
  (4:5–9).

Wisdom is the eternal possession of God.
Solomon was the wisest man of his day and
perhaps of all history. He regarded wisdom as
the greatest need of mankind. Although it is
given by God, it must be diligently sought as
life's most valuable treasure. Its excellent
characteristics are illustrated even by God's tiny

creatures. Rulers, nobles, and judges are among
its prominent clients. It pays great dividends
such as life, longevity, security, and wealth to
those who find it. Its profitable companions are
prudence, knowledge, and discretion. Only a
fool would reject life's principal prize—wisdom.

Wisdom Belongs to God

The LORD possessed me at the beginning
   of His way,
Before His works of old.
I have been established from everlasting,
From the beginning, before there was ever an
   earth.
When there were no depths I was brought forth,
When there were no fountains abounding with
   water.
Before the mountains were settled,
Before the hills, I was brought forth;
While as yet He had not made the earth
   or the fields,
Or the primeval dust of the world.
When He prepared the heavens, I was there,
When He drew a circle on the face of the deep,
When He established the clouds above,
When He strengthened the fountains of the
   deep,
When He assigned to the sea its limit,
So that the waters would not transgress
   His command,

When He marked out the foundations of the
    earth,
Then I was beside Him, as a master craftsman;
And I was daily His delight,
Rejoicing always before Him,
Rejoicing in His inhabited world,
And my delight was with the sons of men
    (8:22–31).

The LORD by wisdom founded the earth;
By understanding He established the heavens;
By His knowledge the depths were broken up,
And clouds drop down the dew (3:19–20).

Wisdom Must Be Sought

My son, if you receive my words,
And treasure my commands within you,
So that you incline your ear to wisdom,
And apply your heart to understanding;
Yes, if you cry out for discernment,
And lift up your voice for understanding,
If you seek her as silver,
And search for her as for hidden treasures;
Then you will understand the fear of the LORD
And find the knowledge of God.
For the LORD gives wisdom;
From His mouth come knowledge and
    understanding (2:1–6).

People Need Wisdom

Wisdom calls aloud outside;
She raises her voice in the open squares.

She cries out in the chief concourses,
At the openings of the gates in the city she
   speaks her words:
"How long, you simple ones, will you love
   simplicity?
For scorners delight in their scorning,
And fools hate knowledge." (1:20–22).

Does not wisdom cry out,
And understanding lift up her voice?
She takes her stand on the top of the high hill,
Beside the way, where the paths meet.
She cries out by the gates,
At the entry of the city,
At the entrance of the doors:
"To you, O men, I call,
And my voice is to the sons of men.
O you simple ones, understand prudence,
And you fools, be of an understanding heart.
Listen, for I will speak of excellent things,
And from the opening of my lips will come
   right things;
For my mouth will speak truth;
Wickedness is an abomination to my lips.
All the words of my mouth are with
   righteousness;
Nothing crooked or perverse is in them.
They are all plain to him who understands,
And right to those who find knowledge.
Receive my instruction, and not silver,
And knowledge rather than choice gold;
For wisdom is better than rubies,

And all the things one may desire cannot be
   compared with her." (8:1–11).

Wisdom has built her house,
She has hewn out her seven pillars;
She has slaughtered her meat,
She has mixed her wine,
She has also furnished her table.
She has sent out her maidens,
She cries out from the highest places of the city,
"Whoever is simple, let him turn in here!"
As for him who lacks understanding, she says
   to him,
"Come, eat of my bread
And drink of the wine which I have mixed.
Forsake foolishness and live,
And go in the way of understanding." (9:1–6).

Wisdom Is Valuable

Receive my instruction, and not silver,
And knowledge rather than choice gold;
For wisdom is better than rubies,
And all the things one may desire cannot be
   compared with her (8:10–11).

Happy is the man who finds wisdom,
And the man who gains understanding;
For her proceeds are better than the profits of
   silver,
And her gain than fine gold.
She is more precious than rubies,

And all the things you may desire cannot
   compare with her.
Length of days is in her right hand,
In her left hand riches and honor.
Her ways are ways of pleasantness,
And all her paths are peace.
She is a tree of life to those who take hold of
   her,
And happy are all who retain her (3:13–18).

How much better it is to get wisdom than gold!
And to get understanding is to be chosen rather
   than silver (16:16).

My son, eat honey because it is good,
And the honeycomb which is sweet to your
   taste;
So shall the knowledge of wisdom be to your
   soul;
If you have found it, there is a prospect,
And your hope will not be cut off (24:13–14).

Wisdom Has Excellent Characteristics
Listen, for I will speak of excellent things,
And from the opening of my lips will come
   right things;
For my mouth will speak truth;
Wickedness is an abomination to my lips.
All the words of my mouth are with
   righteousness;
Nothing crooked or perverse is in them.
They are all plain to him who understands,

And right to those who find knowledge (8:6–9).

"I, wisdom, dwell with prudence,
And find out knowledge and discretion.
The fear of the LORD is to hate evil;
Pride and arrogance and the evil way and the
    perverse mouth I hate.
Counsel is mine, and sound wisdom;
I am understanding, I have strength." (8:12–14).

The words of a man's mouth are deep waters;
The wellspring of wisdom is a flowing brook
    (18:4).

Wisdom Is Illustrated in Nature

There are four things which are little on the
    earth,
But they are exceedingly wise:
The ants are a people not strong,
Yet they prepare their food in the summer;
The rock badgers are a feeble folk,
Yet they make their homes in the crags;
The locusts have no king,
Yet they all advance in ranks;
The spider skillfully grasps with its hands,
And it is in kings' palaces (30:24–28).

Wisdom Has Prominent Clients

By me kings reign,
And rulers decree justice.
By me princes rule, and nobles,
All the judges of the earth (8:15–16).

Wisdom is too lofty for a fool;
He does not open his mouth in the gate (24:7).

Wisdom Pays Dividends

Knowledge

Turn at my reproof;
Surely I will pour out my spirit on you;
I will make my words known to you (1:23).

Life

"Now therefore, listen to me, my children,
For blessed are those who keep my ways.
Hear instruction and be wise,
And do not disdain it.
Blessed is the man who listens to me,
Watching daily at my gates,
Waiting at the posts of my doors.
For whoever finds me finds life,
And obtains favor from the LORD;
But he who sins against me wrongs his own
    soul;
All those who hate me love death." (8:32–36).

He who gets wisdom loves his own soul;
He who keeps understanding will find good
    (19:8).

Longevity

"The fear of the LORD is the beginning of
    wisdom,
And the knowledge of the Holy One is
    understanding.

For by me your days will be multiplied,
And years of life will be added to you.
If you are wise, you are wise for yourself,
And if you scoff, you alone will bear it."
    (9:10–12).

Hear, My son, and receive my sayings,
And the years of your life will be many.
I have taught you in the way of wisdom;
I have led you in right paths.
When you walk, your steps will not be
    hindered,
And when you run, you will not stumble.
Take firm hold of instruction, do not let go;
Keep her, for she is your life (4:10–13).

Morality

When wisdom enters your heart,
And knowledge is pleasant to your soul,
Discretion will preserve you;
Understanding will keep you,
To deliver you from the way of evil,
From the man who speaks perverse things,
From those who leave the paths of uprightness
    to walk in the ways of darkness;
Who rejoice in doing evil,
And delight in the perversity of the wicked;
Whose ways are crooked,
And who are devious in their paths;
To deliver you from the immoral woman,
From the seductress who flatters with her
    words,

Who forsakes the companion of her youth,
And forgets the covenant of her God.
For her house leads down to death,
And her paths to the dead;
None who go to her return,
Nor do they regain the paths of life—
So you may walk in the way of goodness,
And keep to the paths of righteousness.
For the upright will dwell in the land,
And the blameless will remain in it;
But the wicked will be cut off from the earth,
And the unfaithful will be uprooted from it
  (2:10–22).

Say to wisdom, "You are my sister,"
And call understanding your nearest kin,
That they may keep you from the immoral
  woman,
From the seductress who flatters with her words
  (7:4–5).

Security

My son, let them not depart from your eyes—
Keep sound wisdom and discretion;
So they will be life to your soul and grace to
  your neck.
Then you will walk safely in your way,
And your foot will not stumble.
When you lie down, you will not be afraid;
Yes, you will lie down and your sleep will be
  sweet.

Do not be afraid of sudden terror,
Nor of trouble from the wicked when it comes;
For the LORD will be your confidence,
And will keep your foot from being caught
     (3:21–26).

Wealth

Through wisdom a house is built,
And by understanding it is established;
By knowledge the rooms are filled with all
     precious and pleasant riches (24:3–4).

I love those who love me,
And those who seek me diligently will find me.
Riches and honor are with me,
Enduring riches and righteousness.
My fruit is better than gold,
Yes, than fine gold,
And my revenue than choice silver.
I traverse the way of righteousness,
In the midst of the paths of justice,
That I may cause those who love me to inherit
     wealth,
That I may fill their treasuries (8:17–21).

Wisdom Has Profitable Companions

"I, wisdom, dwell with prudence,
And find out knowledge and discretion." (8:12).

Prudence

The wise in heart will be called prudent,
And sweetness of the lips increases learning
     (16:21).

The simple inherit folly,
But the prudent are crowned with knowledge
    (14:18).

The heart of the prudent acquires knowledge,
And the ear of the wise seeks knowledge
    (18:15).

A fool's wrath is known at once,
But a prudent man covers shame (12:16).

Every prudent man acts with knowledge,
But a fool lays open his folly (13:16).

A prudent man conceals knowledge,
But the heart of fools proclaims foolishness
    (12:23).

The wisdom of the prudent is to understand his
    way,
But the folly of fools is deceit (14:8).

The simple believes every word,
But the prudent man considers well his steps
    (14:15).

A prudent man foresees evil and hides himself,
But the simple pass on and are punished (22:3;
    27:12).

A fool despises his father's instruction,
But he who receives reproof is prudent (15:5).

Houses and riches are an inheritance from
    fathers,
But a prudent wife is from the LORD (19:14).

Knowledge

A scoffer seeks wisdom and does not find it,
But knowledge is easy to him who understands
    (14:6).

Also it is not good for a soul to be without
    knowledge,
And he sins who hastens with his feet (19:2).

Discretion

Wise people store up knowledge,
But the mouth of the foolish is near destruction
    (10:14).

As a ring of gold in a swine's snout,
So is a lovely woman who lacks discretion
    (11:22).

The heart of the righteous studies how to
    answer,
But the mouth of the wicked pours forth evil
    (15:28).

The discretion of a man makes him slow to
    anger,
And it is to his glory to overlook a transgression
    (19:11).

Do Not Reject Wisdom

Because I have called and you refused,
I have stretched out my hand and no one
    regarded,
Because you disdained all my counsel,

And would have none of my reproof,
I also will laugh at your calamity;
I will mock when your terror comes,
When your terror comes like a storm,
And your destruction comes like a whirlwind,
When distress and anguish come upon you.
"Then they will call on me, but I will not
    answer;
They will seek me diligently, but they will not
    find me.
Because they hated knowledge
And did not choose the fear of the LORD,
They would have none of my counsel
And despised all my reproof,
Therefore they shall eat the fruit of their own
    way,
And be filled to the full with their own fancies.
For the turning away of the simple will slay
    them,
And the complacency of fools will destroy
    them;
But whoever listens to me will dwell safely,
And will be secure, without fear of evil."
    (1:24–33).

= 3 =

An Excellent Wife Is the Crown of Her Husband

He who finds a wife finds a good thing,
And obtains favor from the LORD (18:22).

Marriage was established by God and is blessed when founded on righteousness and morality. Although Solomon had many wives, his book, the Song of Solomon, reveals that he knew true marital happiness; and his father, David, taught him the dangers of infidelity. Solomon explained that an excellent wife is a gift of great value from God. She brings honor to her husband; she is industrious, talented, attractive, confident, chaste, and worthy of praise or reward. But a foolish wife is a curse; her immorality, hatefulness, contention, destructiveness, and indiscretion bring shame and dishonor.

Marital fidelity should be preserved. Men must escape the enticements of immorality that deceive the simple and bring shame and destruction to its captives. Its paths lead to unfaithfulness, poverty, revenge, ruin, remorse, and death. Wise men avoid such perilous paths and build good marriages on the righteous principles of love and fidelity.

An Excellent Wife Is from God

Houses and riches are an inheritance from
  fathers,
But a prudent wife is from the LORD (19:14).

She Is of Great Value

Who can find a virtuous wife?
For her worth is far above rubies (31:10).

She Honors Her Husband

An excellent wife is the crown of her husband,
But she who causes shame is like rottenness in
  his bones (12:4).

The heart of her husband safely trusts her;
So he will have no lack of gain.
She does him good and not evil
All the days of her life (31:11–12).

Her husband is known in the gates,
When he sits among the elders of the land
  (31:23).

She Has Excellent Characteristics

She watches over the ways of her household,
And does not eat the bread of idleness (31:27).

Industrious

She seeks wool and flax,
And willingly works with her hands (31:13).

She also rises while it is yet night,
And provides food for her household,
And a portion for her maidservants (31:15).

She watches over the ways of her household,
And does not eat the bread of idleness (31:27).

She makes linen garments and sells them,
And supplies sashes for the merchants (31:24).

She considers a field and buys it;
From her profits she plants a vineyard (31:16).

She is not afraid of snow for her household,
For all her household is clothed with scarlet
    (31:21).

Talented

She stretches out her hands to the distaff,
And her hand holds the spindle (31:19).

She makes tapestry for herself;
Her clothing is fine linen and purple (31:22).

She is like the merchant ships,
She brings her food from afar.
She also rises while it is yet night,
And provides food for her household,
And a portion for her maidservants (31:14–15).

Confident

She perceives that her merchandise is good,
And her lamp does not go out by night (31:18).

She Is Morally Excellent

A gracious woman retains honor,
But ruthless men retain riches (11:16).

"Many daughters have done well,
But you excel them all." (31:29).

She girds herself with strength,
And strengthens her arms (31:17).

She opens her mouth with wisdom,
And on her tongue is the law of kindness
 (31:26).

She extends her hand to the poor,
Yes, she reaches out her hands to the needy
 (31:20).

Charm is deceitful and beauty is vain,
But a woman who fears the LORD, she shall be
 praised (31:30).

She Merits Reward

Strength and honor are her clothing;
She shall rejoice in time to come (31:25).

Her children rise up and call her blessed;
Her husband also, and he praises her (31:28).

Give her of the fruit of her hands,
And let her own works praise her in the gates
    (31:31).

A Foolish Wife Is a Curse

She Is Immoral

A foolish woman is clamorous;
She is simple, and knows nothing.
For she sits at the door of her house,
On a seat by the highest places of the city,
To call to those who pass by,
Who go straight on their way:
"Whoever is simple, let him turn in here";
And as for him who lacks understanding, she
    says to him,
"Stolen water is sweet,
And bread eaten in secret is pleasant."
But he does not know that the dead are there,
That her guests are in the depths of hell
    (9:13-18).

She Is Contentious

A foolish son is the ruin of his father,
And the contentions of a wife are a continual
    dripping (19:13).

A continual dripping on a very rainy day
And a contentious woman are alike;
Whoever restrains her restrains the wind,
And grasps oil with his right hand (27:15-16).

It is better to dwell in a corner of a housetop,

Than in a house shared with a contentious
  woman (21:9; 25:24).

It is better to dwell in the wilderness,
Than with a contentious and angry woman
  (21:19).

She Is Destructive

What my son?
And what, son of my womb?
And what, son of my vows?
Do not give your strength to women,
Nor your ways to that which destroys kings
  (31:2–3).

She Is Indiscreet

As a ring of gold in a swine's snout,
So is a lovely woman who lacks discretion
  (11:22).

Preserve Marital Fidelity

Drink water from your own cistern,
And running water from your own well.
Should your fountains be dispersed abroad,
Streams of water in the streets?
Let them be only your own,
And not for strangers with you.
Let your fountain be blessed,
And rejoice with the wife of your youth.
As a loving deer and a graceful doe,
Let her breasts satisfy you at all times;
And always be enraptured with her love.

For why should you, my son, be enraptured by
   an immoral woman,
And be embraced in the arms of a seductress?
   (5:15–20).

Escape Immorality

When wisdom enters your heart,
And knowledge is pleasant to your soul,
Discretion will preserve you;
Understanding will keep you.
To deliver you from the immoral woman,
From the seductress who flatters with her
   words,
Who forsakes the companion of her youth,
And forgets the covenant of her God (2:10–11,
   16–17).

For the commandment is a lamp,
And the law is light;
Reproofs of instruction are the way of life,
To keep you from the evil woman,
From the flattering tongue of a seductress.
Do not lust after her beauty in your heart,
Nor let her allure you with her eyelids.
For by means of a harlot
A man is reduced to a crust of bread;
And an adulteress will prey upon his precious
   life.
Can a man take fire to his bosom,
And his clothes not be burned?
Can one walk on hot coals,
And his feet not be seared?

So is he who goes in to his neighbor's wife;
Whoever touches her shall not be innocent
(6:23–29).

Immorality Entices

To keep you from the evil woman,
From the flattering tongue of a seductress.
Do not lust after her beauty in your heart,
Nor let her allure you with her eyelids
(6:24–25).

For at the window of my house I looked
through my lattice,
And saw among the simple,
I perceived among the youths,
A young man devoid of understanding,
Passing along the street near her corner;
And he took the path to her house in the
twilight,
In the evening,
In the black and dark night.
And there a woman met him,
With the attire of a harlot, and a crafty heart.
She was loud and rebellious,
Her feet would not stay at home.
At times she was outside, at times in the open
square,
Lurking at every corner.
So she caught him and kissed him;
With an impudent face she said to him:
"I have peace offerings with me;
Today I have paid my vows.

So I came out to meet you,
Diligently to seek your face,
And I have found you.
I have spread my bed with tapestry,
Colored coverings of Egyptian linen.
I have perfumed my bed with myrrh, aloes, and
    cinnamon.
Come, let us take our fill of love until morning;
Let us delight ourselves with love.
For my husband is not at home;
He has gone on a long journey;
He has taken a bag of money with him,
And will come home on the appointed day."
With her enticing speech she caused him to
    yield,
With her flattering lips she seduced him
    (7:6–21).

Immorality Deceives

A foolish woman is clamorous;
She is simple, and knows nothing.
For she sits at the door of her house,
On a seat by the highest places of the city,
To call to those who pass by,
Who go straight on their way:
"Whoever is simple, let him turn in here";
And as for him who lacks understanding, she
    says to him,
"Stolen water is sweet,
And bread eaten in secret is pleasant."
But he does not know that the dead are there,

That her guests are in the depths of hell
   (9:13–18).

Immorality Is Shameless

This is the way of an adulterous woman:
She eats and wipes her mouth,
And says, "I have done no wickedness." (30:20).

Immorality Has Dire Consequences

Unfaithfulness

My son, give me your heart,
And let your eyes observe my ways.
For a harlot is a deep pit,
And a seductress is a narrow well.
She also lies in wait as for a victim,
And increases the unfaithful among men
   (23:26–28).

Revenge

People do not despise a thief
If he steals to satisfy himself when he is
   starving.
Yet when he is found, he must restore sevenfold;
He may have to give up all the substance of his
   house.
Whoever commits adultery with a woman lacks
   understanding;
He who does so destroys his own soul.
Wounds and dishonor he will get,
And his reproach will not be wiped away.
For jealousy is a husband's fury;

Therefore he will not spare in the day of
vengeance.
He will accept no recompense,
Nor will he be appeased though you give many
gifts (6:30–35).

Poverty

For by means of a harlot
A man is reduced to a crust of bread;
And an adulteress will prey upon his precious
life.
Can a man take fire to his bosom,
And his clothes not be burned?
Can one walk on hot coals,
And his feet not be seared?
So is he who goes in to his neighbor's wife;
Whoever touches her shall not be innocent
(6:26–29).

Whoever loves wisdom makes his father rejoice,
But a companion of harlots wastes his wealth
(29:3).

Ruin and Remorse

Remove your way far from her,
And do not go near the door of her house,
Lest you give your honor to others,
And your years to the cruel one;
Lest aliens be filled with your wealth,
And your labors go to the house of a foreigner;
And you mourn at last,

When your flesh and your body are consumed,
And say:
"How I have hated instruction,
And my heart despised reproof!
I have not obeyed the voice of my teachers,
Nor inclined my ear to those who instructed
     me!
I was on the verge of total ruin,
In the midst of the congregation and assembly."
     (5:8–14).

The mouth of an immoral woman is a deep pit;
He who is abhorred of the LORD will fall there
     (22:14).

Death

For her house leads down to death,
And her paths to the dead;
None who go to her return,
Nor do they regain the paths of life—
So you may walk in the way of goodness,
And keep to the paths of righteousness
     (2:18–20).

For the lips of an immoral woman drip honey,
And her mouth is smoother than oil;
But in the end she is bitter as wormwood,
Sharp as a two-edged sword.
Her feet go down to death,
Her steps lay hold of hell.
Lest you ponder her path of life—
Her ways are unstable;
You do not know them (5:3–6).

With her enticing speech she caused him to
   yield,
With her flattering lips she seduced him.
Immediately he went after her, as an ox goes to
   the slaughter,
Or as a fool to the correction of the stocks,
Till an arrow struck his liver.
As a bird hastens to the snare,
He did not know it would take his life.
Now therefore, listen to me, my children;
Pay attention to the words of my mouth:
Do not let your heart turn aside to her ways,
Do not stray into her paths;
For she has cast down many wounded,
And all who were slain by her were strong men.
Her house is the way to hell,
Descending to the chambers of death (7:21-27).

4

A Wise Son Makes a Glad Father

Children's children are the crown of old
  men,
And the glory of children is their father
  (17:6).

Solomon viewed the family as the basic
building block of society; it is the material from
which nations are built. God's design specifies
love, honor, and training as the basic
ingredients. Parents and children receive mutual
benefits from one another. Wise parents provide
training for their children's spiritual and
material good. Wise children honor their
parents with obedience and respect, bringing
them happiness and glory. Foolish children
dishonor and defraud their parents, bringing
them sorrow. Such children deserve punishment
and servitude.

Brothers have a tendency to bring adversity.
Hatred and hostility often make poor friends of
brothers. God despises such family discord,

desiring helpful harmony instead.

Wise fathers provide an inheritance for their children. Wise children usually receive a good inheritance, but the foolish inherit the results of their folly.

Godly Parents Benefit Their Children
The righteous man walks in his integrity;
His children are blessed after him (20:7).

They Train Them
Train up a child in the way he should go,
And when he is old he will not depart from it
   (22:6).

They Discipline Them
He who spares his rod hates his son,
But he who loves him disciplines him promptly
   (13:24).

Chasten your son while there is hope,
And do not set your heart on his destruction
   (19:18).

Do not withhold correction from a child,
For if you beat him with a rod, he will not die.
You shall beat him with a rod,
And deliver his soul from hell (23:13–14).

The rod and reproof give wisdom,
But a child left to himself brings shame to his
   mother (29:15).

Correct your son, and he will give you rest;
Yes, he will give delight to your soul (29:17).

They Leave an Inheritance

A good man leaves an inheritance to his
children's children,
But the wealth of the sinner is stored up for the
righteous (13:22).

Wise Children Honor Parents

Whoever loves wisdom makes his father rejoice,
But a companion of harlots wastes his wealth
(29:3).

They Make Parents Happy

A wise son makes a glad father,
But a foolish son is the grief of his mother
(10:1).

A wise son makes a father glad,
But a foolish man despises his mother (15:20).

My son, be wise, and make my heart glad,
That I may answer him who reproaches me
(27:11).

They Obey Parents

A fool despises his father's instruction,
But he who receives reproof is prudent (15:5).

Cease listening to instruction, my son,
And you will stray from the words of
knowledge (19:27).

My son, if your heart is wise,
My heart will rejoice—indeed,I myself;
Yes, my inmost being will rejoice
When your lips speak right things (23:15–16).

The father of the righteous will greatly rejoice,
And he who begets a wise child will delight in
    him.
Let your father and your mother be glad,
And let her who bore you rejoice.
My son, give me your heart,
And let your eyes observe my ways (23:24–26).

Foolish Children Dishonor Parents

A foolish son is a grief to his father,
And bitterness to her who bore him (17:25).

There is a generation that curses its father,
And does not bless its mother (30:11).

They Bring Sorrow

He who begets a scoffer does so to his sorrow,
And the father of a fool has no joy (17:21).

A foolish son is the ruin of his father,
And the contentions of a wife are a continual
    dripping (19:13).

He who mistreats his father and chases away his
    mother
Is a son who causes shame and brings reproach
    (19:26).

Whoever keeps the law is a discerning son,

But a companion of gluttons shames his father
   (28:7).

They Defraud
Whoever robs his father or his mother,
And says, "It is no transgression,"
The same is companion to a destroyer (28:24).

They Deserve Punishment
Whoever curses his father or his mother,
His lamp will be put out in deep darkness
   (20:20).

The eye that mocks his father,
And scorns obedience to his mother,
The ravens of the valley will pick it out,
And the young eagles will eat it (30:17).

They Deserve Servitude
A wise servant will rule over a son who causes
   shame,
And will share an inheritance among the
   brothers (17:2).

A Brother Is Born for Adversity
A friend loves at all times,
And a brother is born for adversity (17:17).

Poor Brother Is Hated
All the brothers of the poor hate him;
How much more do his friends go far from
   him!

He may pursue them with words, yet they
  abandon him (19:7).

Offended Brother Is Hostile

A brother offended is harder to win than a
  strong city,
And contentions are like the bars of a castle
  (18:19).

Brothers Make Bad Friends

A man who has friends must himself be
  friendly,
But there is a friend who sticks closer than a
  brother (18:24).

Do not forsake your own friend or your father's
  friend,
Nor go to your brother's house in the day of
  your calamity;
For better is a neighbor nearby than a brother
  far away (27:10).

God Hates Family Discord

These six things the LORD hates,
Yes, seven are an abomination to Him: . . .
A false witness who speaks lies,
And one who sows discord among brethren
  (6:16, 19).

A Heritage Is from the Father

Houses and riches are an inheritance from
  fathers,

But a prudent wife is from the LORD (19:14).

The Godly Have a Good Inheritance

Whoever causes the upright to go astray in an
    evil way,
He himself will fall into his own pit;
But the blameless will inherit good things
    (28:10).

For the upright will dwell in the land,
And the blameless will remain in it;
But the wicked will be cut off from the earth,
And the unfaithful will be uprooted from it
    (2:21–22).

The wise shall inherit glory,
But shame shall be the legacy of fools (3:35).

That I may cause those who love me to inherit
    wealth,
That I may fill their treasuries (8:21).

Even the Servants Share

A wise servant will rule over a son who causes
    shame,
And will share an inheritance among the
    brothers (17:2).

He who pampers his servant from childhood
Will have him as a son in the end (29:21).

The Foolish Inherit Folly

The simple inherit folly,
But the prudent are crowned with knowledge
(14:18).

He who troubles his own house will inherit the
wind,
And the fool will be servant to the wise of heart
(11:29).

An inheritance gained hastily at the beginning
Will not be blessed at the end (20:21).

=== 5 ===

Train Up a Child

Train up a child in the way he should go,
And when he is old he will not depart
    from it (22:6).

Solomon spoke much about training children. His wisdom has been a successful guide for raising hundreds of generations. It is ironic that his own son rejected his father's training and chose to live foolishly.

Wise training of children requires instruction, correction, and, at times, chastening. Children should be instructed in wisdom and godliness and warned against the dangers of life, such as unlawful gain, unlawful love, indebtedness, and laziness. Correction is necessary by the very nature of children, but it should be properly given with love, purpose, and discernment. When necessary, chastening must be given, but within wise guidelines. The righteous do not need it, but it is sometimes necessary for the less discerning; fools require more. Chastening should inflict some measure of pain and may

need to be harsh in extreme cases; but it serves
as a deterrent to further misbehavior. These
guidelines also apply to chastening administered
by civil authorities. Although the results may be
delayed, training reaps rewards, bringing the
desired results with rest and happiness.

Training Requires Instruction

Hear, my children, the instruction of a father,
And give attention to know understanding;
For I give you good doctrine:
Do not forsake my law.
When I was my father's son,
Tender and the only one in the sight of my
    mother,
He also taught me, and said to me:
"Let your heart retain my words;
Keep my commands, and live." (4:1–4).

Instruct in Godliness

"The fear of the LORD is the beginning of
    wisdom,
And the knowledge of the Holy One is
    understanding." (9:10).

Warn Against Dangers

Against Unlawful Gain

My son, if sinners entice you,
Do not consent.
If they say, "Come with us,

Let us lie in wait to shed blood;
Let us lurk secretly for the innocent without
    cause;
Let us swallow them alive like Sheol,
And whole, like those who go down to the Pit;
We shall find all kinds of precious possessions,
We shall fill our houses with spoil;
Cast in your lot among us,
Let us all have one purse"—
My son, do not walk in the way with them,
Keep your foot from their path;
For their feet run to evil,
And they make haste to shed blood.
Surely, in vain the net is spread in the sight of
    any bird;
But they lie in wait for their own blood,
They lurk secretly for their own lives.
So are the ways of everyone who is greedy for
    gain;
It takes away the life of its owners (1:10–19).

Against Unlawful Love
To deliver you from the immoral woman,
From the seductress who flatters with her
    words,
Who forsakes the companion of her youth,
And forgets the covenant of her God.
For her house leads down to death,
And her paths to the dead;
None who go to her return,
Nor do they regain the paths of life (2:16–19).

Against Unwise Suretyship

My son, if you become surety for your friend,
If you have shaken hands in pledge for a
    stranger,
You are snared by the words of your own
    mouth;
You are taken by the words of your mouth.
So do this, my son, and deliver yourself;
For you have come into the hand of your friend:
Go and humble yourself;
Plead with your friend.
Give no sleep to your eyes,
Nor slumber to your eyelids.
Deliver yourself like a gazelle from the hand of
    the hunter,
And like a bird from the hand of the fowler
    (6:1–5).

Against Laziness

Go to the ant, you sluggard!
Consider her ways and be wise,
Which, having no captain,
Overseer or ruler,
Provides her supplies in the summer,
And gathers her food in the harvest.
How long will you slumber,
O sluggard?
When will you rise from your sleep?
A little sleep, a little slumber,
A little folding of the hands to sleep—
So shall your poverty come on you like a
    robber,

And your need like an armed man (6:6–11).

Training Requires Correction

Correct your son, and he will give you rest;
Yes, he will give delight to your soul (29:17).

Children Need Correction

Foolishness is bound up in the heart of a child,
But the rod of correction will drive it far from
  him (22:15).

The rod and reproof give wisdom,
But a child left to himself brings shame to his
  mother (29:15).

Correction Must be Proper

In Love

My son, do not despise the chastening of the
  LORD,
Nor detest His correction;
For whom the LORD loves He corrects,
Just as a father the son in whom he delights
  (3:11–12).

With Purpose

Do not withhold correction from a child,
For if you beat him with a rod, he will not die.
You shall beat him with a rod,
And deliver his soul from hell (23:13–14).

With Discernment

Do not reprove a scoffer, lest he hate you;
Rebuke a wise man, and he will love you (9:8).

A wise son heeds his father's instruction,
But a scoffer does not listen to rebuke (13:1).

Training Requires Chastening

Chasten your son while there is hope,
And do not set your heart on his destruction
    (19:18).

He who spares his rod hates his son,
But he who loves him disciplines him promptly
    (13:24).

Chastening Has Guidelines

Not for the Righteous

Also, to punish the righteous is not good,
Nor to strike princes for their uprightness
    (17:26).

Necessary for Some

Wisdom is found on the lips of him who has
    understanding,
But a rod is for the back of him who is devoid
    of understanding (10:13).

Judgments are prepared for scoffers,
And beatings for the backs of fools (19:29).

A whip for the horse,
A bridle for the donkey,
And a rod for the fool's back (26:3).

A servant will not be corrected by mere words;
For though he understands, he will not respond
(29:19).

Fools Require More
Reproof is more effective for a wise man
Than a hundred blows on a fool (17:10).

Should Inflict Pain
Blows that hurt cleanse away evil,
As do stripes the inner depths of the heart
(20:30).

Harsh in Extreme Cases
Harsh correction is for him who forsakes the
way,
And he who hates reproof will die (15:10).

Serves as Deterrent
Strike a scoffer, and the simple will become
wary;
Reprove one who has understanding,
and he will discern knowledge (19:25).

Training Reaps Rewards

Train up a child in the way he should go,
And when he is old he will not depart from it
   (22:6).

It Brings Rest

Correct your son, and he will give you rest;
Yes, he will give delight to your soul (29:17).

It Brings Happiness

A wise son makes a father glad,
But a foolish man despises his mother (15:20).

The father of the righteous will greatly rejoice,
And he who begets a wise child will delight in
   him.
Let your father and your mother be glad,
And let her who bore you rejoice (23:24–25).

=6=

A Friend Loves at All Times

A man who has friends must himself be
   friendly,
But there is a friend who sticks closer
   than a brother (18:24).

Because God created man as a social being,
friendship is a vital part of his life. Solomon
found that friends have a strong influence on a
person, therefore a wise man must choose his
friends carefully. True friendship is founded on
love, faithfulness, and honesty; it gives wise
counsel and encouragement. Such friendship is
best found in the congregation of the righteous.
Even so, friends may become fickle, and
friendship may fail in time of need.

Because companionship affects character, one
must avoid corrupt companions such as
flatterers, gluttons, harlots, rebels, and thieves:
these are the companions of fools. In any case,
strangers make comfortless companions.

A wise man makes a good neighbor. He helps in
time of need; he seeks peace, minds his own
business, is truthful and faithful. He does not

57

try to get even, is not a nuisance. On the other
hand, fools make bad neighbors. They despise,
entice to evil, bring harm, and destroy with
slander. A man is blessed who has good friends
and neighbors.

Choose Friends Carefully

The righteous should choose his friends
    carefully,
For the way of the wicked leads them astray
    (12:26).

The father of the righteous will greatly rejoice,
And he who begets a wise child will delight in
    him.
Let your father and mother be glad,
And let her who bore you rejoice (23:24–25).

True Friendship Is Well-Founded

Founded on Love
A friend loves at all times,
And a brother is born for adversity (17:17).

Founded on Faithfulness
Faithful are the wounds of a friend,
But the kisses of an enemy are deceitful (27:6).

Do not forsake your own friend or your father's
    friend,
Nor go to your brother's house in the day of
    your calamity;

For better is a neighbor nearby than a brother
   far away (27:10).

Founded on Counsel
Ointment and perfume delight the heart,
And the sweetness of a man's friend does so by
   hearty counsel (27:9).

Founded on Encouragement
As iron sharpens iron,
So a man sharpens the countenance of his
   friend (27:17).

Friends May Be Fickle

The poor man is hated even by his own
   neighbor,
But the rich has many friends (14:20).

Many entreat the favor of the nobility,
And every man is a friend to one who gives
   gifts (19:6).

Wealth makes many friends,
But the poor is separated from his friend (19:4).

All the brothers of the poor hate him;
How much more do his friends go far from
   him!
He may pursue them with words,
Yet they abandon him (19:7).

Friendship May Fail

A man who isolates himself seeks his own
   desire;
He rages against all wise judgment (18:1).

A perverse man sows strife,
And a whisperer separates the best of friends
   (16:28).

He who covers a transgression seeks love,
But he who repeats a matter separates the best
   of friends (17:9).

Companionship Affects Character

He who walks with wise men will be wise,
But the companion of fools will be destroyed
   (13:20).

Avoid Corrupt Companions

Go from the presence of a foolish man,
When you do not perceive in him the lips of
   knowledge (14:7).

An unjust man is an abomination to the
   righteous,
And he who is upright in the way is an
   abomination to the wicked (29:27).

Avoid Flatterers

He who goes about as a talebearer reveals
   secrets;
Therefore do not associate with one who flatters
   with his lips (20:19).

Avoid Gluttons

Whoever keeps the law is a discerning son,
But a companion of gluttons shames his father
(28:7).

Avoid Harlots

Whoever loves wisdom makes his father rejoice,
But a companion of harlots wastes his wealth
(29:3).

Avoid Rebels

My son, fear the LORD and the king;
Do not associate with those given to change;
For their calamity will rise suddenly,
And who knows the ruin those two can bring?
(24:21-22).

Avoid Thieves

Whoever is a partner with a thief hates his own
life;
He swears to tell the truth,
But reveals nothing (29:24).

Strangers Are Comfortless Companions

The heart knows its own bitterness,
And a stranger does not share its joy (14:10).

A Good Neighbor Is Wise

He Meets Needs

Do not withhold good from those to whom it is
due,

When it is in the power of your hand to do so.
Do not say to your neighbor,
"Go, and come back,
And tomorrow I will give it,"
When you have it with you.
Do not devise evil against your neighbor,
For he dwells by you for safety's sake.
Do not strive with a man without cause,
If he has done you no harm (3:27–30).

He Seeks Peace
Do not go hastily to court;
For what will you do in the end,
When your neighbor has put you to shame?
Debate your case with your neighbor himself,
And do not disclose the secret to another;
Lest he who hears it expose your shame,
And your reputation be ruined (25:8–10).

Minds Own Business
He who passes by and meddles in a quarrel not
    his own
Is like one who takes a dog by the ears (26:17).

Is Truthful
A man who bears false witness against his
    neighbor
Is like a club, a sword, and a sharp arrow
    (25:18).

Like a madman who throws firebrands, arrows,
    and death,
Is the man who deceives his neighbor,

And says,"I was only joking!" (26:18–19).

A man who flatters his neighbor
Spreads a net for his feet (29:5).

The first one to plead his cause seems right,
Until his neighbor comes and examines him
(18:17).

Is Faithful

Do not forsake your own friend or your father's
friend,
Nor go to your brother's house in the day of
your calamity;
For better is a neighbor nearby than a brother
far away (27:10).

Does Not Requite

Do not be a witness against your neighbor
without cause,
For would you deceive with your lips?
Do not say,"I will do to him just as he has done
to me;
I will render to the man according to his
work."(24:28–29).

Is Not a Nuisance

Seldom set foot in your neighbor's house,
Lest he become weary of you and hate you
(25:17).

He who blesses his friend with a loud voice,
rising early in the morning,
It will be counted a curse to him (27:14).

Fools Are Bad Neighbors

They Despise

He who is devoid of wisdom despises his
   neighbor,
But a man of understanding holds his peace
   (11:12).

The poor man is hated even by his own
   neighbor,
But the rich has many friends.
He who despises his neighbor sins;
But he who has mercy on the poor,
Happy is he (14:20–21).

They Entice

A violent man entices his neighbor,
And leads him in a way that is not good
   (16:29).

They Harm

The soul of the wicked desires evil;
His neighbor finds no favor in his eyes (21:10).

They Destroy

The hypocrite with his mouth destroys his
   neighbor,
But through knowledge the righteous will be
   delivered. (11:9).

=== 7 ===

Righteousness Exalts a Nation

The king establishes the land by justice,
But he who receives bribes overthrows it
   (29:4).

Next to family, friends, and church, civil government influences life for good or bad. Solomon's long experience as a ruler taught him that righteousness enhances good government, and a neglect of righteousness leads to governmental chaos. Not only should government promote righteousness, but the rulers themselves should practice it. They should be truthful, merciful, sober, impartial and just. They should be qualified for their positions, exhibiting wisdom, understanding and popular support. Their awesome authority includes the power of life and death, but they must never forget that such authority comes from the sovereign God who holds them responsible.

Unfortunately rulers are vulnerable to such dangers as scheming people and persistent persuasion; therefore, they should follow sound principles of wisdom in the performance of their duties. They should encourage excellence, reward wisdom, deter wickedness, and follow wise counsel. May God bless mankind with such kind rulers.

Righteousness Enhances Good Government

When it goes well with the righteous, the city
   rejoices;
And when the wicked perish, there is shouting.
By the blessing of the upright the city is exalted,
But it is overthrown by the mouth of the wicked
   (11:10–11).

Righteousness exalts a nation,
But sin is a reproach to any people (14:34).

When the righteous rejoice,
There is great glory;
But when the wicked arise,
Men hide themselves. . . .
When they perish,
The righteous increase (28:12, 28).

Rulers Should Be Righteous

It is an abomination for kings to commit
   wickedness,
For a throne is established by righteousness.
Righteous lips are the delight of kings,
And they love him who speaks what is right
   (16:12–13).

When the righteous are in authority,
The people rejoice;
But when a wicked man rules,
The people groan (29:2).

Like a roaring lion and a charging bear
Is a wicked ruler over poor people (28:15).

Truthful
Excellent speech is not becoming to a fool,
Much less lying lips to a prince (17:7).

If a ruler pays attention to lies,
All his servants become wicked (29:12).

The king who judges the poor with truth,
His throne will be established forever (29:14).

Merciful
Mercy and truth preserve the king,
And by lovingkindness he upholds his throne
(20:28).

Sober
It is not for kings,
O Lemuel,
It is not for kings to drink wine,
Nor for princes intoxicating drink;
Lest they drink and forget the law,
And pervert the justice of all the afflicted
(31:4-5).

Impartial

To show partiality is not good,
Because for a piece of bread a man will
    transgress (28:21).

Just

Even though divination is on the lips of the
    king,
His mouth must not transgress in judgment
    (16:10).

A king who sits on the throne of judgment
Scatters all evil with his eyes (20:8).

It is the glory of God to conceal a matter,
But the glory of kings is to search out a matter
    (25:2).

Open your mouth for the speechless,
In the cause of all who are appointed to die.
Open your mouth, judge righteously,
And plead the cause of the poor and needy
    (31:8–9).

Rulers Should Be Qualified

Luxury is not fitting for a fool,
Much less for a servant to rule over princes
    (19:10).

Wise

"I, wisdom, dwell with prudence
And find out knowledge and discretion.
Counsel is mine, and sound wisdom;

I am understanding, I have strength.
By me kings reign,
And rulers decree justice.
By me princes rule, and nobles,
All the judges of the earth" (8:12, 14–16).

Have Understanding

A ruler who lacks understanding is a great
  oppressor,
But he who hates covetousness will prolong his
  days (28:16).

Have Popular Support

In a multitude of people is a king's honor,
But in the lack of people is the downfall of a
  prince (14:28).

Have Authority

My son, fear the LORD and the king;
Do not associate with those given to change
  (24:21).

Rulers Have the Power of Life and Death

As messengers of death is the king's wrath,
But a wise man will appease it.
In the light of the king's face is life,
And his favor is like a cloud of the latter rain
  (16:14–15).

The king's wrath is like the roaring of a lion,
But his favor is like dew on the grass (19:12).

The wrath of a king is like the roaring of a lion;
Whoever provokes him to anger sins against his
  own life. (20:2).

Rulers Are Under God's Sovereignty

The king's heart is in the hand of the LORD,
Like the rivers of water;
He turns it wherever He wishes (21:1).

Many seek the ruler's favor,
But justice for man comes from the LORD
  (29:26).

Rulers Are Vulnerable

As the heavens for height and the earth for
  depth,
So the heart of kings is unsearchable (25:3).

To Schemers
What, my son?
And what, son of my womb?
And what, son of my vows?
Do not give your strength to women,
Nor your ways to that which destroys kings
  (31:2–3).

To Persistent Persuasion
By long forbearance a ruler is persuaded,
And a gentle tongue breaks a bone (25:15).

Rulers Should Follow Wise Principles

Encourage Excellence

Do you see a man who excels in his work?
He will stand before kings;
He will not stand before unknown men (22:29).

Reward Wisdom

The king's favor is toward a wise servant,
But his wrath is against him who causes shame
(14:35).

Deter Wickedness

A wise king sifts out the wicked,
And brings the threshing wheel over them
(20:26).

Take away the dross from silver,
And it will go to the silversmith for jewelry.
Take away the wicked from before the king,
And his throne will be established in
righteousness (25:4–5).

When the wicked are multiplied,
Transgression increases;
But the righteous will see their fall (29:16).

Because of the transgression of a land, many are
its princes;
But by a man of understanding and knowledge
Right will be prolonged (28:2).

=== 8 ===

Labor Produces Profit

The labor of the righteous leads to life,
The wages of the wicked to sin (10:16).

Solomon was a hard worker and observed the folly of laziness. He discovered that the wisdom of hard work is the secret of success in every area of life, from family to government. On the other hand, slothfulness is the folly that leads to failure. Hard work is profitable for sustenance, wealth, and life itself; it develops leadership and good reputation; it must take priority over comfort and leisure. Hunger is often a good incentive for hard work, but vain overwork is unwise because it wastes valuable energy on fleeting fancies.

Slothfulness destroys trust and is a sign of ignorance; it invents excuses for failure and wastes worthy resources. Slothfulness leads its clients into trouble, such as poverty, forced labor, self-neglect, and ultimately to self-destruction. The hard working wise man is far from it.

Diligent Labor Is Wise

Be diligent to know the state of your flocks,
And attend to your herds;
For riches are not forever,
Nor does a crown endure to all generations.
When the hay is removed,
And the tender grass shows itself,
And the herbs of the mountains are gathered in,
The lambs will provide your clothing,
And the goats the price of a field;
You shall have enough goats' milk for your
    food,
For the food of your household,
And the nourishment of your maidservants
    (27:23–27).

Hard Work Is Profitable

He who deals with a slack hand becomes poor,
But the hand of the diligent makes one rich.
He who gathers in summer is a wise son,
But he who sleeps in harvest is a son who
    causes shame (10:4–5).

The labor of the righteous leads to life,
The wages of the wicked to sin (10:16).

He who tills his land will be satisfied with
    bread,
But he who follows frivolity is devoid of
    understanding (12:11).

Wealth gained by dishonesty will be diminished,
But he who gathers by labor will increase
    (13:11).

Where no oxen are, the trough is clean;
But much increase comes by the strength of an
    ox (14:4).

He who tills his land will have plenty of bread,
But he who follows frivolity will have poverty
    enough! (28:19).

Develops Leadership
The hand of the diligent will rule,
But the slothful will be put to forced labor
    (12:24).

Develops Reputation
Do you see a man who excels in his work?
He will stand before kings;
He will not stand before unknown men (22:29).

Requires Priorities
Prepare your outside work,
Make it fit for yourself in the field;
And afterward build your house (24:27).

Hunger Is an Incentive
The person who labors, labors for himself,
For his hungry mouth drives him on (16:26).

Vain Overwork Is Unwise
Do not overwork to be rich;
Because of your own understanding, cease!

Will you set your eyes on that which is not?
For riches certainly make themselves wings;
They fly away like an eagle toward heaven
    (23:4–5).

Slothfulness Is Foolish

As a door turns on its hinges,
So does the slothful turn on his bed.
The sluggard is wiser in his own eyes,
Than seven men who can answer sensibly
    (26:14, 16).

An Offense to Trust

As vinegar to the teeth and smoke to the eyes,
So is the sluggard to those who send him
    (10:26).

A Sign of Ignorance

He who tills his land will be satisfied with
    bread,
But he who follows frivolity is devoid of
    understanding (12:11).

Full of Excuses

The slothful man says,
"There is a lion outside!
I shall be slain in the streets!" (22:13).

The slothful man says,
"There is a lion in the road!
A fierce lion is in the streets!" (26:13).

Wasteful

The slothful man does not roast what he took
    in hunting,
But diligence is man's precious possession
    (12:27).

Much food is in the fallow ground of the poor,
And for lack of justice there is waste (13:23).

He who is slothful in his work
Is a brother to him who is a great destroyer
    (18:9).

Slothfulness Leads to Trouble

The way of the slothful man is like a hedge of
    thorns,
But the way of the upright is a highway (15:19).

Leads to Poverty

Go to the ant, you sluggard!
Consider her ways and be wise,
Which, having no captain,
Overseer or ruler,
Provides her supplies in the summer,
And gathers her food in the harvest.
How long will you slumber, O sluggard?
When will you rise from your sleep?
A little sleep, a little slumber,
A little folding of the hands to sleep—
So shall your poverty come on you like a
    robber,
And your need like an armed man (6:6–11).

He who deals with a slack hand becomes poor,
But the hand of the diligent makes one rich
(10:4).

The soul of a sluggard desires, and has nothing;
But the soul of the diligent shall be made rich
(13:4).

Slothfulness casts one into a deep sleep,
And an idle person will suffer hunger (19:15).

The sluggard will not plow because of winter;
Therefore he will beg during the harvest and
have nothing (20:4).

I went by the field of the slothful,
And by the vineyard of the man devoid of
understanding;
And there it was,
All overgrown with thorns;
Its surface was covered with nettles;
Its stone wall was broken down.
When I saw it, I considered it well;
I looked on it and received instruction:
A little sleep, a little slumber,
A little folding of the hands to rest;
So your poverty will come like a prowler,
And your want like an armed man (24:30–34).

He who tills his land will have plenty of bread,
But he who follows frivolity will have poverty
enough! (28:19).

Leads to Forced Labor

The hand of the diligent will rule,
But the slothful will be put to forced labor
    (12:24).

Leads to Self-Neglect

A slothful man buries his hand in the bowl,
And will not so much as bring it to his mouth
    again (19:24).

The slothful man buries his hand in the bowl;
It wearies him to bring it back to his mouth
    (26:15).

Leads to Self-Destruction

The desire of the slothful kills him,
For his hands refuse to labor.
He covets greedily all day long,
But the righteous gives and does not spare
    (21:25–26).

$$=== 9 ===$$

The Crown of the Wise Is Their Riches

The blessing of the LORD makes one rich,
And He adds no sorrow with it (10:22).

Solomon became one of the world's wealthiest men, and he shared with the wise his secrets for acquiring wealth. Through wisdom and hard work one may acquire wealth with the help of God, family, and friends. Wise methods for increasing wealth consist of diligence, honest labor, righteous character, humility, and seeking the blessing of God. Such blessings are rewards for generosity to others and for honoring God by faithful stewardship of earth's substances. Wealth may also come through an inheritance from a wise father.

But wealth is often squandered through foolishness. Such waste is brought about by wickedness, slothfulness, debt and oppression, dishonesty, extortion, immorality, and drunkenness. Wealth is placed in danger by unwise indebtedness.

Although wealth provides such advantages as strength, power of life, friends, and heritage, it may also lead into trouble; the rich have the tendency of being harsh, overly dominant, and proud. Wealth is found also to be transitory, temporal, and untrustworthy. To the wise many things are more valuable than wealth, such as love, righteousness, humility, honesty, quietness, reputation, integrity, knowledge, understanding, and faithfulness. None of these enduring qualities should be sacrificed for temporal gain.

Wisdom Increases Wealth

Length of days is in her right hand,
In her left hand riches and honor (3:16).

"Riches and honor are with me,
Enduring riches and righteousness." (8:18).

The crown of the wise is their riches,
But the foolishness of fools is folly (14:24).

There is desirable treasure,
And oil in the dwelling of the wise,
But a foolish man squanders it (21:20).

Through wisdom a house is built,
And by understanding it is established;
By knowledge the rooms are filled
With all precious and pleasant riches (24:3-4).

Through Diligence

He who deals with a slack hand becomes poor,
But the hand of the diligent makes one rich.
He who gathers in summer is a wise son,
But he who sleeps in harvest is a son who
    causes shame (10:4–5).

The plans of the diligent lead surely to plenty,
But those of everyone who is hasty,
Surely to poverty (21:5).

Through Honest Labor

Wealth gained by dishonesty will be diminished,
But he who gathers by labor will increase
    (13:11).

In all labor there is profit,
But idle chatter leads only to poverty (14:23).

Through Righteousness

In the house of the righteous there is much
    treasure,
But in the revenue of the wicked is trouble
    (15:6).

Through Humility

By humility and the fear of the LORD
Are riches and honor and life (22:4).

Through God's Blessings

The blessing of the LORD makes one rich,
And He adds no sorrow with it (10:22).

The rich and the poor have this in common,
The LORD is the maker of them all (22:2).

Through Generosity

There is one who makes himself rich,
Yet has nothing;
And one who makes himself poor,
Yet has great riches (13:7).

Through Stewardship

Honor the LORD with your possessions,
And with the firstfruits of all your increase;
So your barns will be filled with plenty,
And your vats will overflow with new wine
   (3:9–10).

Through Inheritance

A good man leaves an inheritance to his
   children's children,
But the wealth of the sinner is stored up for the
   righteous (13:22).

Houses and riches are an inheritance from
   fathers,
But a prudent wife is from the LORD (19:14).

Folly Destroys Wealth

Luxury is not fitting for a fool,
Much less for a servant to rule over princes
   (19:10).

Through Wickedness

Treasures of wickedness profit nothing,
But righteousness delivers from death (10:2).

He who trusts in his riches will fall,
But the righteous will flourish like foliage
(11:28).

A good man leaves an inheritance to his
children's children,
But the wealth of the sinner is stored up for the
righteous (13:22).

Through Slothfulness
He who deals with a slack hand becomes poor,
But the hand of the diligent makes one rich
(10:4).

The soul of a sluggard desires, and has nothing;
But the soul of the diligent shall be made rich
(13:4).

Through Debt
The rich rules over the poor,
And the borrower is servant to the lender
(22:7).

Through Greed
My son, if sinners entice you,
Do not consent.
If they say, "Come with us,
Let us lie in wait to shed blood;
Let us lurk secretly for the innocent without
cause;
Let us swallow them alive like Sheol,
And whole, like those who go down to the Pit;
We shall find all kinds of precious possessions,

We shall fill our houses with spoil;
Cast in your lot among us,
Let us all have one purse"—
My son, do not walk in the way with them,
Keep your foot from their path;
For their feet run to evil,
And they make haste to shed blood.
Surely, in vain the net is spread
In the sight of any bird;
But they lie in wait for their own blood,
They lurk secretly for their own lives.
So are the ways of everyone who is greedy for
    gain;
It takes away the life of its owners (1:10–19).

A faithful man will abound with blessings,
But he who hastens to be rich will not go
    unpunished (28:20).

A man with an evil eye hastens after riches,
And does not consider that poverty will come
    upon him (28:22).

Through Oppressing the Poor
He who oppresses the poor to increase his
    riches,
And he who gives to the rich, will surely come
    to poverty (22:16).

Through Dishonesty
Wealth gained by dishonesty will be diminished,
But he who gathers by labor will increase
    (13:11).

Getting treasures by a lying tongue
Is the fleeting fantasy of those who seek death
     (21:6).

Through Extortion

One who increases his possessions by usury and
     extortion
Gathers it for him who will pity the poor
     (28:8).

Through Immorality

Whoever loves wisdom makes his father rejoice,
But a companion of harlots wastes his wealth
     (29:3).

Through Drunkenness

He who loves pleasure will be a poor man;
He who loves wine and oil will not be rich
     (21:17).

Wealth Provides Advantages

Provides Strength

The rich man's wealth is his strong city;
The destruction of the poor is their poverty
     (10:15).

The rich man's wealth is his strong city,
And like a high wall in his own esteem (18:11).

Provides Power

The ransom of a man's life is his riches,
But the poor does not hear rebuke (13:8).

Provides Friends

The poor man is hated even by his own
    neighbor,
But the rich has many friends (14:20).

Wealth makes many friends,
But the poor is separated from his friend (19:4).

Provides Heritage

Houses and riches are an inheritance from
    fathers,
But a prudent wife is from the LORD (19:14).

Wealth May Lead to Trouble

He who is greedy for gain troubles his own
    house,
But he who hates bribes will live (15:27).

To Harshness

The poor man uses entreaties,
But the rich answers roughly (18:23).

To Dominance

The rich rules over the poor,
And the borrower is servant to the lender
    (22:7).

To Pride

The rich man is wise in his own eyes,
But the poor who has understanding searches
    him out (28:11).

Wealth Has Limitations

It Is Transitory

Will you set your eyes on that which is not?
For riches certainly make themselves wings;
They fly away like an eagle toward heaven
    (23:5).

It Is Temporal

For riches are not forever,
Nor does a crown endure to all generations
    (27:24).

Riches do not profit in the day of wrath,
But righteousness delivers from death (11:4).

It Is Not Trustworthy

He who trusts in his riches will fall,
But the righteous will flourish like foliage
    (11:28).

Many Things Are Better Than Wealth

Love Is Better

Better is a little with the fear of the LORD,
Than great treasure with trouble.
Better is a dinner of herbs where love is,
Than a fatted calf with hatred (15:16–17).

Righteousness Is Better

Better is a little with righteousness,
Than vast revenues without justice (16:8).

Better is the poor who walks in his integrity
Than one perverse in his ways, though he be
    rich (28:6).

Humility Is Better

Better to be of a humble spirit with the lowly,
Than to divide the spoil with the proud (16:19).

By humility and the fear of the LORD
Are riches and honor and life (22:4).

Honesty Is Better

Two things I request of You
(Deprive me not before I die):
Remove falsehood and lies far from me;
Give me neither poverty nor riches—
Feed me with the food You prescribe for me;
Lest I be full and deny You,
And say, "Who is the LORD?"
Or lest I be poor and steal,
And profane the name of my God (30:7–9).

Quietness Is Better

Better is a dry morsel with quietness,
Than a house full of feasting with strife (17:1).

Reputation Is Better

A good name is to be chosen rather than great
    riches,
Loving favor rather than silver and gold (22:1).

Integrity Is Better

Better is the poor who walks in his integrity
Than one perverse in his ways, though he be
  rich (28:6).

Knowledge Is Better

Receive my instruction, and not silver,
And knowledge rather than choice gold (8:10).

There is gold and a multitude of rubies,
But the lips of knowledge are a precious jewel
  (20:15).

Understanding Is Better

How much better it is to get wisdom than gold!
And to get understanding is to be chosen rather
  than silver (16:16).

Faithfulness Is Better

A faithful man will abound with blessings,
But he who hastens to be rich will not go
  unpunished (28:20).

Suretyship Endangers Wealth

A man devoid of understanding shakes hands in
  a pledge,
And becomes surety for his friend (17:18).

My son, if you become surety for your friend,
If you have shaken hands in pledge for a
  stranger,
You are snared by the words of your own
  mouth;

You are taken by the words of your mouth.
So do this, my son,
And deliver yourself;
For you have come into the hand of your friend:
Go and humble yourself;
Plead with your friend.
Give no sleep to your eyes,
Nor slumber to your eyelids.
Deliver yourself like a gazelle from the hand of
    the hunter,
And like a bird from the hand of the fowler
    (6:1–5).

Do not be one of those who shakes hands in a
    pledge,
One of those who is surety for debts;
If you have nothing with which to pay,
Why should he take away your bed from under
    you? (22:26–27).

He who is surety for a stranger will suffer for it,
But one who hates being surety is secure
    (11:15).

Take the garment of one who is surety for a
    stranger,
And hold it as a pledge when it is for a
    seductress (20:16; 27:13).

=== 10 ===

The Foolishness of Fools Is Folly

> Folly is joy to him who is destitute of
>   discernment,
> But a man of understanding walks up-
>   rightly (15:21).

Folly is the antithesis of wisdom; it destroys
anyone who follows it. Solomon often warned
against following after folly. Because the human
heart is naturally inclined toward folly, it is
easily enticed by folly's seductive appeal. But
folly leads to adversity that results in
destruction, servitude, sin, shame, and
punishment. It brings the miseries of bitterness,
grief, sorrow, and ruin. It transforms its
followers into scoffers, mockers, perverted and
impetuous persons, and oppressors. The wise
man avoids folly as a contagious disease.

Folly Is a Seductress
For at the window of my house I looked
   through my lattice,
And saw among the simple,
I perceived among the youths,

A young man devoid of understanding,
Passing along the street near her corner;
And he took the path to her house
In the twilight, in the evening,
In the black and dark night.
And there a woman met him,
With the attire of a harlot,
And a crafty heart.
She was loud and rebellious,
Her feet would not stay at home.
At times she was outside,
At times in the open square,
Lurking at every corner.
So she caught him and kissed him;
With an impudent face she said to him:
"I have peace offerings with me;
Today I have paid my vows.
So I came out to meet you,
Diligently to seek your face,
And I have found you.
I have spread my bed with tapestry,
Colored coverings of Egyptian linen.
I have perfumed my bed
With myrrh, aloes, and cinnamon.
Come, let us take our fill of love until morning;
Let us delight ourselves with love.
For my husband is not at home;
He has gone on a long journey;
He has taken a bag of money with him,
And will come home on the appointed day."
With her enticing speech she caused him to
    yield,

With her flattering lips she seduced him.
Immediately he went after her,
As an ox goes to the slaughter,
Or as a fool to the correction of the stocks,
Till an arrow struck his liver.
As a bird hastens to the snare,
He did not know it would take his life.
Now therefore, listen to me, my children;
Pay attention to the words of my mouth:
Do not let your heart turn aside to her ways,
Do not stray into her paths;
For she has cast down many wounded,
And all who were slain by her were strong men.
Her house is the way to hell,
Descending to the chambers of death (7:6–27).

A foolish woman is clamorous;
She is simple, and knows nothing.
For she sits at the door of her house,
On a seat by the highest places of the city,
To call to those who pass by,
Who go straight on their way:
"Whoever is simple,
Let him turn in here";
And as for him who lacks understanding,
She says to him,
"Stolen water is sweet,
And bread eaten in secret is pleasant."
But he does not know that the dead are there,
That her guests are in the depths of hell
    (9:13–18).

Folly Leads to Adversity

Wisdom calls aloud outside;
She raises her voice in the open squares. . . .
"I also will laugh at your calamity;
I will mock when your terror comes." (1:20, 26).

To Destruction

The wise in heart will receive commands,
But a prating fool will fall.
He who winks with the eye causes trouble,
But a prating fool will fall (10:8, 10).

To Servitude

He who troubles his own house will inherit the
    wind,
And the fool will be servant to the wise of heart
    (11:29).

To Sin

The devising of foolishness is sin,
And the scoffer is an abomination to men
    (24:9).

To Shame

The wise shall inherit glory,
But shame shall be the legacy of fools (3:35).

To Punishment

Judgments are prepared for scoffers,
And beatings for the backs of fools (19:29).

A whip for the horse,
A bridle for the donkey,

And a rod for the fool's back (26:3).

Folly Brings Misery

Bitterness

A foolish son is a grief to his father,
And bitterness to her who bore him (17:25).

Grief

The Proverbs of Solomon:
A wise son makes a glad father,
But a foolish son is the grief of his mother
     (10:1).

Ruin

A foolish son is the ruin of his father,
And the contentions of a wife are a continual
     dripping (19:13).

Sorrow

He who begets a scoffer does so to his sorrow,
And the father of a fool has no joy (17:21).

Fools Have Dreadful Companions

He who walks with wise men will be wise,
But the companion of fools will be destroyed
     (13:20).

Scoffers

A scoffer seeks wisdom and does not find it,
But knowledge is easy to him who understands
     (14:6).

A scoffer does not love one who reproves him,
Nor will he go to the wise (15:12).

A proud and haughty man—
"Scoffer" is his name;
He acts with arrogant pride (21:24).

He who begets a scoffer does so to his sorrow,
And the father of a fool has no joy (17:21).

He who plots to do evil will be called a
   schemer.
The devising of foolishness is sin,
And the scoffer is an abomination to men
   (24:8–9).

Scoffers ensnare a city,
But wise men turn away wrath (29:8).

Strike a scoffer, and the simple will become
   wary;
Reprove one who has understanding,
And he will discern knowledge (19:25).

When the scoffer is punished,
The simple is made wise;
But when the wise is instructed,
He receives knowledge (21:11).

Cast out the scoffer,
And contention will leave;
Yes, strife and reproach will cease (22:10).

Judgments are prepared for scoffers,
And beatings for the backs of fools (19:29).

Mockers

To do evil is like sport to a fool,
But a man of understanding has wisdom
   (10:23).

Fools mock at sin,
But among the upright there is favor (14:9).

He who mocks the poor reproaches his Maker;
He who is glad at calamity will not go
   unpunished (17:5).

Wine is a mocker, intoxicating drink arouses
   brawling,
And whoever is led astray by it is not wise
   (20:1).

The eye that mocks his father,
And scorns obedience to his mother,
The ravens of the valley will pick it out,
And the young eagles will eat it (30:17).

Perverse Persons

Thorns and snares are in the way of the
   perverse;
He who guards his soul will be far from them
   (22:5).

He who walks in his uprightness fears the LORD,
But he who is perverse in his ways despises Him
   (14:2).

The foolishness of a man twists his way,
And his heart frets against the LORD (19:3).

Whoever walks blamelessly will be saved,
But he who is perverse in his ways will fall at
  once (28:18).

A wholesome tongue is a tree of life,
But perverseness in it breaks the spirit (15:4).

The way of a guilty man is perverse;
But as for the pure,
His work is right (21:8).

A man will be commended according to his
  wisdom,
But he who is of a perverse heart will be
  despised (12:8).

He who walks with integrity walks securely,
But he who perverts his ways will become
  known (10:9).

He who has a deceitful heart finds no good,
And he who has a perverse tongue falls into evil
  (17:20).

Who has woe? Who has sorrow?
Who has contentions? Who has complaints?
Who has wounds without cause?
Who has redness of eyes?
Those who linger long at the wine,
Those who go in search of mixed wine.
Do not look on the wine when it is red,
When it sparkles in the cup,
When it swirls around smoothly;
At the last it bites like a serpent,
And stings like a viper.

Your eyes will see strange things,
And your heart will utter perverse things
(23:29–33).

Better is the poor who walks in his integrity
Than one who is perverse in his lips, and is a
fool (19:1).

Better is the poor who walks in his integrity
Than one perverse in his ways, though he be
rich (28:6).

The integrity of the upright will guide them,
But the perversity of the unfaithful will destroy
them (11:3).

Put away from you a deceitful mouth,
And put perverse lips far from you (4:24).

Impetuous Persons
These six things the LORD hates,
Yes, seven are an abomination to Him. . . .
A heart that devises wicked plans,
Feet that are swift in running to evil (6:16, 18).

He who answers a matter before he hears it,
It is folly and shame to him (18:13).

Do you see a man hasty in his words?
There is more hope for a fool than for him
(29:20).

Also it is not good for a soul to be without
knowledge,
And he sins who hastens with his feet (19:2).

An inheritance gained hastily at the beginning
Will not be blessed at the end (20:21).

Do not go hastily to court;
For what will you do in the end,
When your neighbor has put you to shame?
Debate your case with your neighbor himself,
And do not disclose the secret to another;
Lest he who hears it expose your shame,
And your reputation be ruined (25:8–10).

The plans of the diligent lead surely to plenty,
But those of everyone who is hasty, surely to
    poverty (21:5).

A faithful man will abound with blessings,
But he who hastens to be rich will not go
    unpunished.
A man with an evil eye hastens after riches,
And does not consider that poverty will come
    upon him (28:20, 22).

Oppressors
He who oppresses the poor reproaches his
    Maker,
But he who honors Him has mercy on the
    needy (14:31).

A poor man who oppresses the poor
Is like a driving rain which leaves no food
    (28:3).

A ruler who lacks understanding is a great
    oppressor,

But he who hates covetousness will prolong his
days (28:16).

The poor man and the oppressor have this in
common:
The LORD gives light to the eyes of both (29:13).

He who oppresses the poor to increase his
riches,
And he who gives to the rich,
Will surely come to poverty.
Do not rob the poor because he is poor,
Nor oppress the afflicted at the gate;
For the LORD will plead their cause,
And plunder the soul of those who plunder
them (22:16, 22–23).

Do not lie in wait, O wicked man,
Against the dwelling of the righteous;
Do not plunder his resting place;
For a righteous man may fall seven times and
rise again,
But the wicked shall fall by calamity (24:15–16).

═ 11 ═

Fools Hate Knowledge

Wisdom is too lofty for a fool;
He does not open his mouth in the gate
(24:7).

In an attempt to turn men away from folly,
Solomon taught the traits of fools that must be
avoided by the wise.

Fools are the followers of folly. Being committed
to this way of life leaves them virtually
incapable of wisdom. This fateful frame of mind
develops the terrible traits that set them on the
path of self-destruction. Fools exhibit the traits
of boastfulness, complacency, perversity, and
wickedness. They clamor, chatter, and slander.
They are spiteful, destructive, dishonorable,
hostile, ignorant, treacherous and vicious, hasty
and impulsive. They are careless, self-righteous
and quarrelsome. They are unstable, unreliable,
unbearable, unreasonable, unrestrained, and
untruthful. They cannot discern and cannot be
corrected or taught. Such traits are an
abomination to God and a disgrace to man.

Wise men flee far from them.

Fools Have Terrible Traits

The lips of the righteous feed many,
But fools die for lack of wisdom (10:21).

Boastfulness

Do not boast about tomorrow,
For you do not know what a day may bring
     forth (27:1).

Complacency

For the turning away of the simple will slay
     them,
And the complacency of fools will destroy them
     (1:32).

Perversity

The foolishness of a man twists his way,
And his heart frets against the LORD (19:3).

Wickedness

A worthless person, a wicked man,
Walks with a perverse mouth;
He winks with his eyes,
He shuffles his feet,
He points with his fingers;
Perversity is in his heart,
He devises evil continually,
He sows discord.
Therefore his calamity shall come suddenly;

Suddenly he shall be broken without remedy
(6:12–15).

The Tongues of Fools Practice Evil

Clamor

A foolish woman is clamorous;
She is simple, and knows nothing (9:13).

Chatter

The tongue of the wise uses knowledge rightly,
But the mouth of fools pours forth foolishness.
The heart of him who has understanding seeks
knowledge,
But the mouth of fools feeds on foolishness
(15:2, 14).

Slander

Whoever hides hatred has lying lips,
And whoever spreads slander is a fool (10:18).

Fools Are Corrupt in Many Ways

Spiteful

A wise son makes a father glad,
But a foolish man despises his mother (15:20).

Destructive

Every wise woman builds her house,
But the foolish pulls it down with her hands
(14:1).

A fool's mouth is his destruction,
And his lips are the snare of his soul (18:7).

Dishonorable

As snow in summer and rain in harvest,
So honor is not fitting for a fool.
Like one who binds a stone in a sling
Is he who gives honor to a fool (26:1, 8).

Hostile

A stone is heavy and sand is weighty,
But a fool's wrath is heavier than both of them
(27:3).

Ignorant

"How long, you simple ones,
Will you love simplicity?
For scorners delight in their scorning,
And fools hate knowledge." (1:22).

He shall die for lack of instruction,
And in the greatness of his folly he shall go
astray (5:23).

Every prudent man acts with knowledge,
But a fool lays open his folly (13:16).

Go from the presence of a foolish man,
When you do not perceive in him the lips of
knowledge (14:7).

The lips of the wise disperse knowledge,
But the heart of the fool does not do so (15:7).

A fool has no delight in understanding,
But in expressing his own heart (18:2).

Surely I am more stupid than any man,

And do not have the understanding of a man.
I neither learned wisdom
Nor have knowledge of the Holy One (30:2–3).

Treacherous

Let a man meet a bear robbed of her cubs,
Rather than a fool in his folly (17:12).

Vicious

There is a generation whose teeth are like
    swords,
And whose fangs are like knives,
To devour the poor from off the earth,
And the needy from among men (30:14).

Hasty

He who answers a matter before he hears it,
It is folly and shame to him (18:13).

Impulsive

He who is slow to wrath has great
    understanding,
But he who is impulsive exalts folly (14:29).

Careless

A wise man fears and departs from evil,
But a fool rages and is self-confident (14:16).

He who trusts in his own heart is a fool,
But whoever walks wisely will be delivered
    (28:26).

Self-Righteous

The way of a fool is right in his own eyes,
But he who heeds counsel is wise (12:15).

Quarrelsome

A fool's lips enter into contention,
And his mouth calls for blows (18:6).

It is honorable for a man to stop striving,
Since any fool can start a quarrel (20:3).

Unstable

Like a bird that wanders from its nest
Is a man who wanders from his place (27:8).

Unreliable

He who sends a message by the hand of a fool
Cuts off his own feet and drinks violence (26:6).

Unbearable

For three things the earth is perturbed,
Yes, for four it cannot bear up:
For a servant when he reigns,
A fool when he is filled with food,
A hateful woman when she is married,
And a maidservant who succeeds her mistress
     (30:21–23).

If a wise man contends with a foolish man,
Whether the fool rages or laughs,
There is no peace (29:9).

Unreasonable
Do not answer a fool according to his folly,
Lest you also be like him.
Answer a fool according to his folly,
Lest he be wise in his own eyes (26:4–5).

Unrestrained
A fool vents all his feelings,
But a wise man holds them back (29:11).

A fool's wrath is known at once,
But a prudent man covers shame (12:16).

Wisdom rests quietly in the heart of him who
    has understanding,
But what is in the heart of fools is made known
    (14:33).

Untruthful
The wisdom of the prudent is to understand his
    way,
But the folly of fools is deceit (14:8).

Fools Cannot Discern
Like the legs of the lame that hang limp
Is a proverb in the mouth of fools.
Like a thorn that goes into the hand of a
    drunkard
Is a proverb in the mouth of fools (26:7, 9).

Folly is joy to him who is destitute of
  discernment,
But a man of understanding walks uprightly
  (15:21).

Do not speak in the hearing of a fool,
For he will despise the wisdom of your words
  (23:9).

Fools Cannot Be Corrected

As a dog returns to his own vomit,
So a fool repeats his folly (26:11).

Reproof is more effective for a wise man
Than a hundred blows on a fool (17:10).

Fools Cannot Be Taught

A fool despises his father's instruction,
But he who receives reproof is prudent (15:5).

Why is there in the hand of a fool the purchase
  price of wisdom,
Since he has no heart for it? (17:16).

Though you grind a fool in a mortar with a
  pestle along with crushed grain,
Yet his foolishness will not depart from him
  (27:22).

The fear of the LORD is the beginning of
  knowledge,
But fools despise wisdom and instruction (1:7).

=== 12 ===

Wrath Is Cruel and Anger a Torrent

> A stone is heavy and sand is weighty,
> But a fool's wrath is heavier than both of
> them (27:3).

As a wise judge, Solomon often had to deal with wrath and anger, strife and contention. These problems arise from folly, but they may be calmed and controlled by wisdom. Among other things, anger is aroused by backbiting. Anger stirs up trouble, produces strife, causes failure, and at times leads to death; yet it may be quieted by wisdom, turned aside by a soft answer, or pacified by a gift. Men of discretion learn to control their temper; this enables them to relieve contention. This is a much better tactic than using force to stop a fight.

Strife is often stirred up by sins such as hatred, wrath, whispering, contention, and pride; it is far worse than poverty. But strife may be stopped by terminating the talebearing, by excluding the scoffer, or by separating the scrappers, but not without difficulty and even danger.

Contention creates catastrophic conditions that are usually caused by foolish things such as pride, scoffing, or drunkenness, but it can sometimes be calmed by such a simple thing as drawing straws. Wise men are peacemakers and will choose loneliness rather than a life of contention.

Anger Is Foolish

A fool's wrath is known at once,
But a prudent man covers shame (12:16).

He who is quick-tempered acts foolishly,
And a man of wicked intentions is hated
(14:17).

Anger Is Aroused by Backbiting

The north wind brings forth rain,
And a backbiting tongue an angry countenance
(25:23).

Anger Arouses Trouble

A man of great wrath will suffer punishment;
For if you deliver him,
You will have to do it again (19:19).

Produces Strife

For as the churning of milk produces butter,
And as wringing the nose produces blood,

So the forcing of wrath produces strife (30:33).

Causes Failure
He who sows iniquity will reap sorrow,
And the rod of his anger will fail (22:8).

Leads to Death
The wrath of a king is like the roaring of a lion;
Whoever provokes him to anger sins against his
　　own life (20:2).

As messengers of death is the king's wrath,
But a wise man will appease it (16:14).

Anger May Be Quieted

Quieted by Wisdom
Scoffers ensnare a city,
But wise men turn away wrath (29:8).

Quieted by Soft Answers
A soft answer turns away wrath,
But a harsh word stirs up anger (15:1).

Quieted by Gifts
A gift in secret pacifies anger,
And a bribe behind the back, strong wrath
　　(21:14).

But Not Always
Riches do not profit in the day of wrath,
But righteousness delivers from death (11:4).

Controlled Temper Is Wise

He who is slow to wrath has great
understanding,
But he who is impulsive exalts folly (14:29).

It Allays Contention
A wrathful man stirs up strife,
But he who is slow to anger allays contention
(15:18).

Is Better Than Might
He who is slow to anger is better than the
mighty,
And he who rules his spirit than he who takes a
city (16:32).

Produced by Discretion
The discretion of a man makes him slow to
anger,
And it is to his glory to overlook a transgression
(19:11).

Strife Is Stirred Up by Sin

He who loves transgression loves strife,
And he who exalts his gate seeks destruction
(17:19).

Caused by Hatred
Hatred stirs up strife,
But love covers all sins (10:12).

Caused by Wrath

An angry man stirs up strife,
And a furious man abounds in transgression
    (29:22).

Caused by Whispering

A perverse man sows strife,
And a whisperer separates the best of friends
    (16:28).

Caused by Contention

As charcoal is to burning coals, and wood to
    fire,
So is a contentious man to kindle strife (26:21).

Caused by Pride

He who is of a proud heart stirs up strife,
But he who trusts in the LORD will be prospered
    (28:25).

Perpetuated by Talebearing

Where there is no wood, the fire goes out;
And where there is no talebearer, strife ceases
    (26:20).

The words of a talebearer are like tasty trifles,
And they go down into the inmost body
    (26:22).

Worse Than Poverty

Better is a dry morsel with quietness,
Than a house full of feasting with strife (17:1).

Strife May Be Stopped

It is honorable for a man to stop striving,
Since any fool can start a quarrel (20:3).

By Separating the Scoffer
Cast out the scoffer, and contention will leave;
Yes, strife and reproach will cease (22:10).

But with Difficulty and Danger
The beginning of strife is like releasing water;
Therefore stop contention before a quarrel starts
(17:14).

He who passes by and meddles in a quarrel not
his own
Is like one who takes a dog by the ears (26:17).

Contention Creates Catastrophe

A brother offended is harder to win than a
strong city,
And contentions are like the bars of a castle
(18:19).

A foolish son is the ruin of his father,
And the contentions of a wife are a continual
dripping (19:13).

A continual dripping on a very rainy day
And a contentious woman are alike;
Whoever restrains her restrains the wind,
And grasps oil with his right hand (27:15–16).

Contention Caused By Folly

A fool's lips enter into contention,
And his mouth calls for blows (18:6).

Caused by Pride

By pride comes only contention,
But with the well-advised is wisdom (13:10).

Caused by Scoffing

Diverse weights and diverse measures,
They are both alike, an abomination to the
    Lord (20:10).

Caused by Drinking

Who has woe?
Who has sorrow?
Who has contentions?
Who has complaints?
Who has wounds without cause?
Who has redness of eyes?
Those who linger long at the wine,
Those who go in search of mixed wine
    (23:29–30).

Contention Can Cease

Casting lots causes contentions to cease,
And keeps the mighty apart (18:18).

Loneliness Is Better

It is better to dwell in a corner of a housetop,
Than in a house shared with a contentious
    woman. (21:9)

It is better to dwell in the wilderness,
Than with a contentious and angry woman
    (21:19).

Make no friendship with an angry man.
And with a furious man do not go,
Lest you learn his ways and set a snare for your
    soul (22:24–25).

═ 13 ═

Wine Is a Mocker

> He who loves pleasure will be a poor
>   man;
> He who loves wine and oil will not be
>   rich (21:17).

Intoxicating drink has been a social and moral problem from antiquity. Solomon spoke of its dangers for the individual in his personal life, in his social life, and in civil government. For the individual, drinking produces violence, raging temper, poverty, sorrow, misery and addiction. In one's social contacts, there is the social pressure to drink on the one hand and the danger of social disgrace on the other. For civil rulers, drinking should be forbidden because it leads to the miscarriage of justice. Although in ancient times alcoholic drink had some medical value for those in extreme physical or emotional pain, modern medicine has provided far superior relief. The wise man avoids all the dangers of alcoholic drink.

Intoxicating Drink Produces Many Problems

Who has woe?
Who has sorrow?
Who has contentions?
Who has complaints?
Who has wounds without cause?
Who has redness of eyes?
Those who linger long at the wine,
Those who go in search of mixed wine
    (23:29–30).

Raging Temper

Wine is a mocker, intoxicating drink arouses
    brawling,
And whoever is led astray by it is not wise
    (20:1).

Poverty

For the drunkard and the glutton will come to
    poverty,
And drowsiness will clothe a man with rags
    (23:21).

Sorrow and Misery

Your eyes will see strange things,
And your heart will utter perverse things.
Yes, you will be like one who lies down in the
    midst of the sea,
Or like one who lies at the top of the mast,
    saying:
"They have struck me, but I was not hurt;

They have beaten me, but I did not feel it."
  (23:33–35a).

Addiction
"When shall I awake, that I may seek another
  drink?" (23:35b).

The Social Pressure to Drink
Hear, my son, and be wise;
And guide your heart in the way.
Do not mix with winebibbers,
Or with gluttonous eaters of meat (23:19–20).

Do not look on the wine when it is red,
When it sparkles in the cup,
When it swirls around smoothly (23:31).

Social Disgrace
At the last it bites like a serpent,
And stings like a viper (23:32).

Civil Dangers
It is not for kings, O Lemuel,
It is not for kings to drink wine,
Nor for princes intoxicating drink;
Lest they drink and forget the law,
And pervert the justice of all the afflicted
  (31:4–5).

Wine Is for the Desperate

Give strong drink to him who is perishing,
And wine to those who are bitter of heart.

Let him drink and forget his poverty,
And remember his misery no more (31:6–7).

= 14 =

The Destruction of the Poor Is Their Poverty

The poor man is hated even by his own
  neighbor,
But the rich has many friends.
He who despises his neighbor sins;
But he who has mercy on the poor, happy
  is he (14:20–21).

Poverty is the perpetual problem of mankind.
"The poor you have with you always" (John
12:8); but the poor are the object of God's
interest: "Blessed are you poor, for yours is the
kingdom of God" (Luke 6:20). Solomon
observed that God pities the poor and makes
them the object of mercy. The poor have need
of good government to provide them with just
protection from oppression.

Poverty has a destructive effect; it tends to drive
away friends, to destroy one's independence,
and to undermine integrity. Yet poverty is often
the product of a person's own bad habits. It
may be brought on by willful ignorance, by

miserliness, wickedness, idle chatter,
impulsiveness, drunkenness, frivolity,
extravagance, and especially by pure laziness.

Nevertheless, poverty is preferable to those
things that are morally unwise, such as pride,
perverseness, untruthfulness, wickedness, and
even strife.

God Pities the Poor

Do not rob the poor because he is poor,
Nor oppress the afflicted at the gate;
For the LORD will plead their cause,
And plunder the soul of those who plunder
 them (22:22–23).

One who increases his possessions by usury and
 extortion
Gathers it for him who will pity the poor
 (28:8).

He who gives to the poor will not lack,
But he who hides his eyes will have many curses
 (28:27).

The poor man and the oppressor have this in
 common:
The LORD gives light to the eyes of both (29:13).

The LORD will destroy the house of the proud,
But He will establish the boundary of the
 widow (15:25).

He who mocks the poor reproaches his Maker;

He who is glad at calamity will not go
   unpunished (17:5).

He who has pity on the poor lends to the LORD,
And He will pay back what he has given
   (19:17).

The Poor Need Mercy

The poor man is hated even by his own
   neighbor,
But the rich has many friends.
He who despises his neighbor sins;
But he who has mercy on the poor, happy is he
   (14:20-21).

He who oppresses the poor reproaches his
   Maker,
But he who honors Him has mercy on the
   needy (14:31).

Whoever shuts his ears to the cry of the poor
Will also cry himself and not be heard (21:13).

He who has a bountiful eye will be blessed,
For he gives of his bread to the poor (22:9).

The righteous considers the cause of the poor,
But the wicked does not understand such
   knowledge (29:7).

The poor man uses entreaties,
But the rich answers roughly (18:23).

The Poor Need Justice in Government

The king who judges the poor with truth,
His throne will be established forever (29:14).

Open your mouth for the speechless,
In the cause of all who are appointed to die.
Open your mouth, judge righteously,
And plead the cause of the poor and needy
  (31:8–9).

Poverty Destroys

The rich man's wealth is his strong city;
The destruction of the poor is their poverty
  (10:15).

Destroys Friendship

Wealth makes many friends,
But the poor is separated from his friend (19:4).

All the brothers of the poor hate him;
How much more do his friends go far from
  him!
He may pursue them with words, yet they
  abandon him (19:7).

Destroys Independence

The rich rules over the poor,
And the borrower is servant to the lender
  (22:7).

Destroys Integrity

Two things I request of You
(Deprive me not before I die):

Remove falsehood and lies far from me;
Give me neither poverty nor riches—
Feed me with the food You prescribe for me;
Lest I be full and deny You,
And say, "Who is the LORD"
Or lest I be poor and steal,
And profane the name of my God (30:7-9).

Poor Practices Produce Poverty

Poverty and shame will come to him who
   disdains correction,
But he who regards reproof will be honored
   (13:18).

By Willful Ignorance

The ransom of a man's life is his riches,
But the poor does not hear rebuke (13:8).

By Miserliness

There is one who scatters, yet increases more;
And there is one who withholds more than is
   right,
But it leads to poverty (11:24).

There is one who makes himself rich, yet has
   nothing;
And one who makes himself poor, yet has great
   riches (13:7).

By Wickedness

The righteous eats to the satisfying of his soul,
But the stomach of the wicked shall be in want
   (13:25).

By Idle Chatter

In all labor there is profit,
But idle chatter leads only to poverty (14:23).

By Impulsiveness

The plans of the diligent lead surely to plenty,
But those of everyone who is hasty, surely to
   poverty (21:5).

A man with an evil eye hastens after riches,
And does not consider that poverty will come
   upon him (28:22).

By Drinking

Hear, my son, and be wise;
And guide your heart in the way.
Do not mix with winebibbers,
Or with gluttonous eaters of meat;
For the drunkard and the glutton will come to
   poverty,
And drowsiness will clothe a man with rags
   (23:19–21).

By Frivolity

He who tills his land will have plenty of bread,
But he who follows frivolity will have poverty
   enough!(28:19).

He who loves pleasure will be a poor man;
He who loves wine and oil will not be rich
   (21:17).

By Extravagance

He who oppresses the poor to increase his
   riches,
And he who gives to the rich, will surely come
   to poverty (22:16).

By Slothfulness

Go to the ant, you sluggard!
Consider her ways and be wise,
Which, having no captain, overseer or ruler,
Provides her supplies in the summer,
And gathers her food in the harvest.
How long will you slumber, O sluggard?
When will you rise from your sleep?
A little sleep, a little slumber,
A little folding of the hands to sleep—
So shall your poverty come on you like a
   robber,
And your need like an armed man (6:6–11).

He who deals with a slack hand becomes poor,
But the hand of the diligent makes one rich.
He who gathers in summer is a wise son,
But he who sleeps in harvest is a son who
   causes shame (10:4–5).

Much food is in the fallow ground of the poor,
And for lack of justice there is waste (13:23).

Where no oxen are, the trough is clean;
But much increase comes by the strength of an
ox (14:4).

Slothfulness casts one into a deep sleep,
And an idle person will suffer hunger (19:15).

The sluggard will not plow because of winter;
Therefore he will beg during the harvest and
have nothing (20:4).

Do not love sleep, lest you come to poverty;
Open your eyes, and you will be satisfied with
bread (20:13).

I went by the field of the slothful,
And by the vineyard of the man devoid of
understanding;
And there it was, all overgrown with thorns;
Its surface was covered with nettles;
Its stone wall was broken down.
When I saw it, I considered it well;
I looked on it and received instruction:
A little sleep, a little slumber,
A little folding of the hands to rest;
So your poverty will come like a prowler,
And your want like an armed man (24:30–34).

Poverty May Be Preferable

A poor man who oppresses the poor
Is like a driving rain which leaves no food
(28:3).

Preferable to Pride

Better is the one who is slighted but has a
    servant,
Than he who honors himself but lacks bread
    (12:9).

The rich man is wise in his own eyes,
But the poor who has understanding searches
    him out (28:11).

Better to be of a humble spirit with the lowly,
Than to divide the spoil with the proud (16:19).

Preferable to Perverseness

Better is the poor who walks in his integrity
Than one who is perverse in his lips, and is a
    fool (19:1).

Better is the poor who walks in his integrity
Than one perverse in his ways, though he be
    rich (28:6).

Preferable to Untruthfulness

What is desired in a man is kindness,
And a poor man is better than a liar (19:22).

Preferable to Wickedness

Better is a little with the fear of the LORD,
Than great treasure with trouble.
Better is a dinner of herbs where love is,
Than a fatted calf with hatred (15:16–17).

Better is a little with righteousness,
Than vast revenues without justice (16:8).

Preferable to Strife

Better is a dry morsel with quietness,
Than a house full of feasting with strife (17:1).

= 15 =

Give Instruction to a Wise Man

> Receive my instruction, and not silver,
> And knowledge rather than choice gold
> (8:10).

Solomon knew the great value of instruction, reproof, and correction to those who receive them. He indicated that instruction is a source of knowledge and wisdom that is of lasting value. It is available from numerous sources, such as God's Word, parents, wisdom, teachers, counselors, and even from the failures of fools. The wise readily receive instruction, but fools reject it.

Reproof also is profitable; it provides such benefits as honor, knowledge, and understanding. The wise readily receive reproof, but fools refuse it, with dire consequences.

In addition, correction is profitable to the wise but of little value to fools. In case of continued disobedience, correction may require harshness; but obedience is the wisest response, because it provides such benefits as longevity, wisdom, and understanding. By contrast, disobedience often results in punishment, poverty, and even the ruination of prayers. Wise men welcome instruction, reproof, and correction, knowing that they bring blessings and benefits.

Instruction Is Profitable

Incline your ear and hear the words of the wise,
And apply your heart to my knowledge;
For it is a pleasant thing if you keep them
    within you;
Let them all be fixed upon your lips,
So that your trust may be in the LORD;
I have instructed you today, even you.
Have I not written to you excellent things
Of counsels and knowledge,
That I may make you know the certainty of the
    words of truth,
That you may answer words of truth to those
    who send to you? (22:17–21).

Buy the truth, and do not sell it,
Also wisdom and instruction and understanding
    (23:23).

He who disdains instruction despises his own
    soul,
But he who heeds reproof gets understanding.
The fear of the LORD is the instruction of
    wisdom,
And before honor is humility (15:32–33).

Instruction Provides Knowledge

Whoever loves instruction loves knowledge,
But he who hates reproof is stupid (12:1).

The heart of him who has understanding seeks
knowledge,
But the mouth of fools feeds on foolishness
(15:14).

Cease listening to instruction, my son,
And you will stray from the words of
knowledge (19:27).

Apply your heart to instruction,
And your ears to words of knowledge (23:12).

Instruction Provides Wisdom

Listen to counsel and receive instruction,
That you may be wise in your latter days
(19:20).

Hear instruction and be wise,
And do not disdain it (8:33).

Instruction Has Lasting Value

Train up a child in the way he should go,
And when he is old he will not depart from it
(22:6).

Instruction Is Available

From God's Word

The proverbs of Solomon the son of David,
    king of Israel:
To know wisdom and instruction,
To perceive the words of understanding (1:1–2).

From Parents

My son, hear the instruction of your father,
And do not forsake the law of your mother;
For they will be graceful ornaments on your
    head,
And chains about your neck (1:8–9).

Hear, my children, the instruction of a father
And give attention to know understanding (4:1).

From Wisdom

To receive the instruction of wisdom,
Justice, judgment, and equity (1:3).

"Receive my instruction, and not silver,
And knowledge rather than choice gold." (8:10).

From Teachers

I have not obeyed the voice of my teachers,
Nor inclined my ear to those who instructed
    me! (5:13).

From Counselors

Listen to counsel and receive instruction,
That you may be wise in your latter days
    (19:20).

From the Failure of Fools

I went by the field of the slothful,
And by the vineyard of the man devoid of
  understanding;
And there it was, all overgrown with thorns;
Its surface was covered with nettles;
Its stone wall was broken down.
When I saw it, I considered it well;
I looked on it and received instruction:
A little sleep, a little slumber,
A little folding of the hands to rest;
So your poverty will come like a prowler,
And your want like an armed man (24:30–34).

The Wise Receive Instruction

A wise son heeds his father's instruction,
But a scoffer does not listen to rebuke (13:1).

When the scoffer is punished, the simple is
  made wise;
But when the wise is instructed, he receives
  knowledge (21:11).

Give instruction to a wise man, and he will be
  still wiser;
Teach a just man, and he will increase in
  learning (9:9).

Take firm hold of instruction, do not let go;
Keep her, for she is your life (4:13).

Fools Reject Instruction

The fear of the LORD is the beginning of
  knowledge,
But fools despise wisdom and instruction (1:7).

A fool despises his father's instruction,
But he who receives reproof is prudent (15:5).

He who disdains instruction despises his own
  soul,
But he who heeds reproof gets understanding
  (15:32).

Why is there in the hand of a fool the purchase
  price of wisdom,
Since he has no heart for it? (17:16).

Reproof Is Profitable

A word fitly spoken is like apples of gold
In settings of silver.
Like an earring of gold and an ornament of fine
  gold
Is a wise reprover to an obedient ear (25:11–12).

He who rebukes a man will find more favor
  afterward
Than he who flatters with the tongue (28:23).

Provides Honor

Poverty and shame will come to him who
  disdains correction,
But he who regards reproof will be honored
  (13:18).

Provides Knowledge

Strike a scoffer, and the simple will become
  wary;
Reprove one who has understanding, and he
  will discern knowledge (19:25).

Provides Understanding

The ear that hears the reproof of life
Will abide among the wise.
He who disdains instruction despises his own
  soul,
But he who heeds reproof gets understanding
  (15:31–32).

The Wise Receive Reproof

He who reproves a scoffer gets shame for
  himself,
And he who rebukes a wicked man gets himself
  a blemish.
Do not reprove a scoffer, lest he hate you;
Rebuke a wise man, and he will love you.
Give instruction to a wise man, and he will still
  be wiser;
Teach a just man, and he will increase in
  learning (9:7–9).

Reproof is more effective for a wise man
Than a hundred blows on a fool (17:10).

Fools Reject Reproof

Whoever loves instruction loves knowledge,
But he who hates reproof is stupid (12:1).

A scoffer does not love one who reproves him,
Nor will he go to the wise (15:12).

With Dire Consequences
Harsh correction is for him who forsakes the
    way,
And he who hates reproof will die (15:10).

He who is often reproved, and hardens his
    neck,
Will suddenly be destroyed, and that without
    remedy (29:1).

Correction Is Profitable
For whom the LORD loves He corrects,
Just as a father the son in whom he delights
    (3:12).

Correct your son, and he will give you rest;
Yes, he will give delight to your soul (29:17).

Buy the truth, and do not sell it,
Also wisdom and instruction and understanding
    (23:23).

Correction Is of Little Profit to Fools
Understanding is a wellspring of life to him who
    has it.
But the correction of fools is folly (16:22).

Do not answer a fool according to his folly,
Lest you also be like him.

Answer a fool according to his folly,
Lest he be wise in his own eyes (26:4-5).

Correction May Require Harshness

Harsh correction is for him who forsakes the
    way,
And he who hates reproof will die (15:10).

A servant will not be corrected by mere words;
For though he understands,
He will not respond (29:19).

Obedience Is Wise

My son, hear the instruction of your father,
And do not forsake the law of your mother;
For they will be graceful ornaments on your
    head,
And chains about your neck (1:8-9).

The wise in heart will receive commands,
But a prating fool will fall (10:8).

Obedience Is Profitable

He who heeds the word wisely will find good,
And whoever trusts in the LORD, happy is he
    (16:20).

It Provides Longevity

Hear, my son, and receive my sayings,
And the years of your life will be many (4:10).

He who keeps the commandment keeps his soul,

But he who is careless of his ways will die
(19:16).

It Provides Wisdom

He who keeps instruction is in the way of life,
But he who refuses reproof goes astray (10:17).

The ear that hears the reproof of life
Will abide among the wise (15:31).

Hear, my son, and be wise;
And guide your heart in the way (23:19).

It Provides Understanding

He who disdains instruction despises his own
soul,
But he who heeds reproof gets understanding
(15:32).

Disobedience Is Unprofitable

It Brings Punishment

The eye that mocks his father,
And scorns obedience to his mother,
The ravens of the valley will pick it out,
And the young eagles will eat it (30:17).

It Brings Poverty

Poverty and shame will come to him who
disdains correction,
But he who regards reproof will be honored
(13:18).

It Ruins Prayer

One who turns away his ear from hearing the
　law,
Even his prayer shall be an abomination (28:9).

=== 16 ===

God Shall Direct Your Paths

A man's heart plans his way,
But the LORD directs his steps (16:9).

In addition to instruction, the wise man is in
need of guidance in preparation for making
plans and decisions. Guidance is also available
from God, from parents, and from wise
counselors and friends. Solomon sought the
guidance of God and the counsel of men on
many occasions; he shared the principles of
decision making with the wise.

Divine guidance is available to those who trust
God to provide it, and who expect it to
accompany wise planning. In addition to His
Word, God guides through circumstances and
the inner perceptions of the heart. For the godly
man who has wisdom, this guidance is reliable;
fools fail to receive or perceive it.

Wise parental guidance also is of great value. It
promises such benefits as longevity, peace, life,
health, discretion, and knowledge. It warns of

the dangers of drinking, and it recommends righteousness.

Counselors and friends may provide guidance, but wisdom and counsel must be mutual partners; and multiple counsel provides a measure of safety. Friendly counsel brings delight to the heart, but the more valuable counsel may need to be drawn from the deep wells of thoughtful reserve.

Counsel from the ungodly is unreliable and unwise, and any counsel against God is powerless and doomed to failure. Wise men seek sound guidance before making plans and decisions.

God Gives Guidance

A man's steps are of the LORD;
How then can a man understand his own way?
    (20:24).

Guidance Comes by Trust

Trust in the LORD with all your heart,
And lean not on your own understanding;
In all your ways acknowledge Him,
And He shall direct your paths (3:5–6).

Commit your works to the LORD,
And your thoughts will be established (16:3).

Guidance Accompanies Plans

The preparations of the heart belong to man,
But the answer of the tongue is from the LORD
   (16:1).

Guidance Comes by Circumstances

The lot is cast into the lap,
But its every decision is from the LORD (16:33).

Guidance Comes by the Heart

The king's heart is in the hand of the LORD,
Like the rivers of water;
He turns it wherever He wishes (21:1).

For the perverse person is an abomination to the
   LORD,
But His secret counsel is with the upright (3:32).

God's Guidance Is Reliable

There are many plans in a man's heart,
Nevertheless the LORD'S counsel—that will stand
   (19:21).

Parents Give Guidance

Listen to your father who begot you,
And do not despise your mother when she is
   old (23:22).

My son, keep your father's command,
And do not forsake the law of your mother.
Bind them continually upon your heart;

Tie them around your neck.
When you roam, they will lead you;
When you sleep, they will keep you;
And when you awake, they will speak with
    you.
For the commandment is a lamp,
And the law is light;
Reproofs of instruction are the way of life
    (6:20–23).

My son, give me your heart,
And let your eyes observe my ways (23:26).

A wise son heeds his father's instruction,
But a scoffer does not listen to rebuke (13:1).

Guidance Is Profitable

My son, hear the instruction of your father,
And do not forsake the law of your mother;
For they will be graceful ornaments on your
    head,
And chains about your neck (1:8–9).

Hear, my children, the instruction of a father,
And give attention to know understanding;
For I give you good doctrine:
Do not forsake my law.
When I was my father's son,
Tender and the only one in the sight of my
    mother,
He also taught me, and said to me:
"Let your heart retain my words;
Keep my commands, and live." (4:1–4).

It Promises Longevity, Peace

My son, do not forget my law,
But let your heart keep my commands;
For length of days and long life
And peace they will add to you (3:1-2).

Hear, my son, and receive my sayings,
And the years of your life will be many.
I have taught you in the way of wisdom;
I have led you in right paths.
When you walk, your steps will not be
    hindered,
And when you run, you will not stumble.
Take firm hold of instruction, do not let go;
Keep her, for she is your life (4:10-13).

It Promises Life, Health

My son, give attention to my words;
Incline your ear to my sayings.
Do not let them depart from your eyes;
Keep them in the midst of your heart;
For they are life to those who find them,
And health to all their flesh (4:20-22).

My son, keep my words,
And treasure my commands within you.
Keep my commands and live,
And my law as the apple of your eye.
Bind them on your fingers;
Write them on the tablet of your heart.
Say to wisdom, "You are my sister,"
And call understanding your nearest kin
    (7:1-4).

It Promises Discretion, Knowledge

My son, pay attention to my wisdom;
Lend your ear to my understanding,
That you may preserve discretion,
And that your lips may keep knowledge.
Therefore hear me now, my children,
And do not depart from the words of my
    mouth (5:1-2, 7).

Incline your ear and hear the words of the wise,
And apply your heart to my knowledge;
For it is a pleasant thing if you keep them
    within you;
Let them all be fixed upon your lips,
So that your trust may be in the LORD;
I have instructed you today, even you.
Have I not written to you excellent things
Of counsels and knowledge,
That I may make you know the certainty of the
    words of truth,
That you may answer words of truth
To those who send to you? (22:17-21).

It Warns Against Drinking

Hear, my son, and be wise;
And guide your heart in the way.
Do not mix with winebibbers,
Or with gluttonous eaters of meat;
For the drunkard and the glutton will come to
    poverty,
And drowsiness will clothe a man with rags
    (23:19-21).

It Recommends Righteousness

The integrity of the upright will guide them,
But the perversity of the unfaithful will destroy
    them.
Riches do not profit in the day of wrath,
But righteousness delivers from death.
The righteousness of the blameless will direct
    his way aright,
But the wicked will fall by his own wickedness.
The righteousness of the upright will deliver
    them,
But the unfaithful will be taken by their own
    lust (11:3-6).

Do not enter the path of the wicked,
And do not walk in the way of evil.
Avoid it, do not travel on it;
Turn away from it and pass on.
For they do not sleep unless they have done
    evil;
And their sleep is taken away unless they make
    someone fall.
For they eat the bread of wickedness,
And drink the wine of violence (4:14-17).

The righteous should choose his friends
    carefully,
For the way of the wicked leads them astray
    (12:26).

Counselors Give Guidance

The way of a fool is right in his own eyes,
But he who heeds counsel is wise (12:15).

Every purpose is established by counsel;
By wise counsel wage war (20:18).

Wisdom Is a Perfect Counselor

"Listen, for I will speak of excellent things,
And from the opening of my lips will come
 right things;
For my mouth will speak truth;
Wickedness is an abomination to my lips.
All the words of my mouth are with
 righteousness;
Nothing crooked or perverse is in them.
They are all plain to him who understands,
And right to those who find knowledge."
 (8:6–9).

Good Counsel Gives Wisdom

By pride comes only contention,
But with the well–advised is wisdom (13:10).

Listen to counsel and receive instruction,
That you may be wise in your latter days
 (19:20).

Incline your ear and hear the words of the wise,
And apply your heart to my knowledge;
For it is a pleasant thing if you keep them
 within you;

Let them all be fixed upon your lips,
So that your trust may be in the LORD;
I have instructed you today, even you.
Have I not written to you excellent things
Of counsels and knowledge,
That I may make you know the certainty of the
    words of truth,
That you may answer words of truth
To those who send to you? (22:17–21).

Multiple Counsel Gives Safety

Where there is no counsel, the people fall;
But in the multitude of counselors there is
    safety (11:14).

Without counsel, plans go awry,
But in the multitude of counselors they are
    established (15:22).

For by wise counsel you will wage your own
    war,
And in a multitude of counselors there is safety
    (24:6).

Friendly Counsel Gives Delight

Ointment and perfume delight the heart,
And the sweetness of a man's friend does so by
    hearty counsel (27:9).

Counsel May Need Drawing Out

Counsel in the heart of man is like deep water,
But a man of understanding will draw it out
  (20:5).

Counsel of the Ungodly Is Unreliable

The thoughts of the righteous are right,
But the counsels of the wicked are deceitful.
The words of the wicked are, "Lie in wait for
  blood,"
But the mouth of the upright will deliver them
  (12:5-6).

A violent man entices his neighbor,
And leads him in a way that is not good
  (16:29).

Counsel Is Powerless Against God

There is no wisdom or understanding
Or counsel against the LORD (21:30).

══ 17 ══

A Man's Heart Plans His Way

> The plans of the diligent lead surely to
> plenty,
> But those of everyone who is hasty, surely
> to poverty (21:5).

Plans are a necessary part of the wise man's life; only fools follow the path of fateful chance. Solomon advised that plans should follow the priority of work before comfort and should be made only after seeking counsel and guidance from God and men. Even God's tiny creature the ant has enough wisdom to plan for winter.

Fools plan wickedness, but such plans are hated and condemned by the general public because they bring only shame to everyone involved. The plans of wise men incorporate righteous principles.

Priorities are important for successful plans; wisdom and work should be at the top of the list. The next priority is the principle of choosing the best quality over that which is merely good or better. Solomon listed numerous

priorities of this type: righteousness is preferable
to ritual or riches; reputation and honesty to
riches; love and quietness to luxury; loneliness
to contention; humility to self-honor;
self-control to power; rebuke to flattery or
concealed love; friendship to familial
dependency.

Proper priorities require right thinking. Several
times Solomon commended right thinking and
warned that wicked thinking is hated. Such
thoughts characterize evil. Wise men avoid
wicked thinking but base their plans on
righteous priorities, wise counsel, and guidance.

Wise Men Plan Ahead

A prudent man foresees evil and hides himself;
The simple pass on and are punished (22:3;
   27:12).

Through wisdom a house is built,
And by understanding it is established;
By knowledge the rooms are filled
With all precious and pleasant riches (24:3–4).

With Priorities

Prepare your outside work,
Make it fit for yourself in the field;
And afterward build your house (24:27).

With Counsel

Without counsel, plans go awry,
But in the multitude of counselors they are
    established (15:22).

With God's Guidance

The preparations of the heart belong to man,
But the answer of the tongue is from the LORD
    (16:1).

There are many plans in a man's heart,
Nevertheless the LORD'S counsel—that will stand
    (19:21).

Even Ants Plan Ahead

There are four things which are little on the
    earth,
But they are exceedingly wise:
The ants are a people not strong,
Yet they prepare their food in the summer
    (30:24–25).

Fools Plan Wickedness

Do not be envious of evil men,
Nor desire to be with them;
For their heart devises violence,
And their lips talk of troublemaking (24:1–2).

Do they not go astray who devise evil?
But mercy and truth belong to those who devise
    good (14:22).

A violent man entices his neighbor,
And leads him in a way that is not good.
He winks his eye to devise perverse things;
He purses his lips and brings about evil
  (16:29–30).

Such Plans Are Hated
These six things the LORD hates,
Yes, seven are an abomination to Him:
A proud look,
A lying tongue,
Hands that shed innocent blood,
A heart that devises wicked plans,
Feet that are swift in running to evil (6:16–18).

He who plots to do evil
Will be called a schemer.
The devising of foolishness is sin,
And the scoffer is an abomination to men
  (24:8–9).

Such Plans Are Condemned
A good man obtains favor from the LORD,
But a man of wicked devices He will condemn
  (12:2).

Such Plans Bring Shame
If you have been foolish in exalting yourself,
Or if you have devised evil, put your hand on
  your mouth (30:32).

Priorities Are Prudent

Listen, for I will speak of excellent things,
And from the opening of my lips will come
  right things (8:6).

Give Priority to Wisdom

"Get wisdom! Get understanding!
Do not forget, nor turn away from the words of
  my mouth.
Do not forsake her, and she will preserve you;
Love her, and she will keep you.
Wisdom is the principal thing;
Therefore get wisdom.
And in all your getting, get understanding.
Exalt her, and she will promote you;
She will bring you honor, when you embrace
  her.
She will place on your head an ornament of
  grace;
A crown of glory she will deliver to you."
  (4:5–9).

For wisdom is better than rubies,
And all the things one may desire cannot be
  compared with her (8:11).

How much better it is to get wisdom than gold!
And to get understanding is to be chosen rather
  than silver (16:16).

Give Priority to Work

Prepare your outside work,
Make it fit for yourself in the field;
And afterward build your house (24:27).

Choose the Best

Righteousness over Ritual

To do righteousness and justice
Is more acceptable to the LORD than sacrifice
(21:3).

Righteousness over Riches

Better is a little with the fear of the LORD,
Than great treasure with trouble (15:16).

Reputation over Riches

A good name is to be chosen rather than great
riches,
Loving favor rather than silver and gold (22:1).

Better is a little with righteousness,
Than vast revenues without justice (16:8).

Honesty over Riches

Better is the poor who walks in his integrity
Than one who is perverse in his lips, and is a
fool (19:1).

What is desired in a man is kindness,
And a poor man is better than a liar (19:22).

Better is the poor who walks in his integrity

Than one perverse in his ways, though he be
  rich (28:6).

Love over Luxury

Better is a dinner of herbs where love is,
Than a fatted calf with hatred (15:17).

Quietness over Luxury

Better is a dry morsel with quietness,
Than a house full of feasting with strife (17:1).

Loneliness over Contention

It is better to dwell in a corner of a housetop,
Than in a house shared with a contentious
  woman (21:9; 25:24).

It is better to dwell in the wilderness,
Than with a contentious and angry woman
  (21:19).

Humility over Self-Honor

Better is the one who is slighted but has a
  servant,
Than he who honors himself but lacks bread
  (12:9).

Do not exalt yourself in the presence of the
  king,
And do not stand in the place of great men;
For it is better that he say to you,
"Come up here,"
Than that you should be put lower in the
  presence of the prince,
Whom your eyes have seen (25:6-7).

Self-Control over Strength

He who is slow to anger is better than the
  mighty,
And he who rules his spirit than he who takes a
  city (16:32).

Rebuke over Flattery

He who rebukes a man will find more favor
  afterward
Than he who flatters with the tongue (28:23).

Rebuke over Concealed Love

Open rebuke is better
Than love carefully concealed (27:5).

Friendship over Familial Dependency

Do not forsake your own friend or your father's
  friend,
Nor go to your brother's house in the day of
  your calamity;
For better is a neighbor nearby than a brother
  far away (27:10).

Think Righteously

The way of a fool is right in his own eyes,
But he who heeds counsel is wise (12:15).

Do they not go astray who devise evil?
But mercy and truth belong to those who devise
  good (14:22).

Wisdom is in the sight of him who has
   understanding,
But the eyes of a fool are on the ends of the
   earth (17:24).

Commit your works to the LORD,
And your thoughts will be established (16:3).

Wicked Thoughts Are Hated

The thoughts of the wicked are an abomination
   to the LORD,
But the words of the pure are pleasant (15:26).

The sacrifice of the wicked is an abomination;
How much more when he brings it with wicked
   intent! (21:27).

He who is quick-tempered acts foolishly,
And a man of wicked intentions is hated
   (14:17).

Wicked Thoughts Characterize Evil

A violent man entices his neighbor,
And leads him in a way that is not good.
He winks his eye to devise perverse things;
He purses his lips and brings about evil
   (16:29–30).

Do not be envious of evil men,
Nor desire to be with them;
For their heart devises violence,
And their lips talk of troublemaking (24:1–2).

Do not eat the bread of a miser,
Nor desire his delicacies;
For as he thinks in his heart, so is he.
"Eat and drink!" He says to you,
But his heart is not with you.
The morsel you have eaten, you will vomit up,
And waste your pleasant words (23:6-8).

=== 18 ===

A Man's Heart Reveals the Inner Man

> The refining pot is for silver and the fur-
>   nace for gold,
> But the LORD tests the hearts (17:3).

A man's spiritual and physical health is greatly
affected by his heart, the inner being. "As he
thinks in his heart, so is he" (23:7). Solomon
said that a sound heart is spiritually healthful.
It helps to control the speech wisely; it aids the
prudent acquisition of knowledge; it has a
purifying influence; and it worships in hope.
A cheerful heart usually contributes to physical
health, but not always. In any case, the heart
reveals the inner man, both to God and to his
own conscience.

Chastening is designed to cleanse the heart,
because the unsound heart is detrimental to
spiritual and physical health. The unsound
heart is exhibited in various forms, such as the
foolish heart, the heavy heart, the broken heart,
the deceitful heart, and the vengeful heart. A

wise man guards the health of his heart; a fool
neglects it to his own downfall.

A Sound Heart Is Healthful

A sound heart is life to the body,
But envy is rottenness to the bones (14:30).

It Wisely Controls Speech

The heart of the wise teaches his mouth,
And adds learning to his lips (16:23).

It Prudently Acquires Knowledge

The heart of the prudent acquires knowledge,
And the ear of the wise seeks knowledge
   (18:15).

It Has Pure Influence

He who loves purity of heart
And has grace on his lips,
The king will be his friend (22:11).

It Worships In Hope

Do not let your heart envy sinners,
But in the fear of the LORD continue all day
   long;
For surely there is a hereafter,
And your hope will not be cut off (23:17–18).

A Cheerful Heart Is Healthful

A merry heart does good, like medicine,
But a broken spirit dries the bones (17:22).

A merry heart makes a cheerful countenance,
But by sorrow of the heart the spirit is broken
    (15:13).

All the days of the afflicted are evil,
But he who is of a merry heart has a continual
    feast (15:15).

The light of the eyes rejoices the heart,
And a good report makes the bones healthy
    (15:30).

Pleasant words are like a honeycomb,
Sweetness to the soul and health to the bones
    (16:24).

But Not Always
Even in laughter the heart may sorrow,
And the end of mirth may be grief (14:13).

The Heart Reveals the Man

As in water face reveals face,
So a man's heart reveals the man (27:19).

To God
Every way of a man is right in his own eyes,
But the LORD weighs the hearts (21:2).

To His Conscience
The spirit of a man is the lamp of the LORD,
Searching all the inner depths of his heart
    (20:27).

Chastening Cleanses the Heart

Blows that hurt cleanse away evil,
As do stripes the inner depths of the heart
(20:30).

An Unsound Heart Is Unhealthy

The Foolish Heart

The foolishness of a man twists his way,
And his heart frets against the LORD (19:3).

Why is there in the hand of a fool the purchase
price of wisdom,
Since he has no heart for it? (17:16).

The Insensitive Heart

Like one who takes away a garment in cold
weather,
And like vinegar on soda,
Is one who sings songs to a heavy heart (25:20).

The Broken Heart

The spirit of a man will sustain him in sickness,
But who can bear a broken spirit? (18:14).

The Deceitful Heart

He who has a deceitful heart finds no good,
And he who has a perverse tongue falls into evil
(17:20).

The Vengeful Heart

Do not rejoice when your enemy falls,
And do not let your heart be glad when he
  stumbles;
Lest the LORD see it, and it displease Him,
And He turn away His wrath from him
  (24:17–18).

=== 19 ===

Love Covers All Sins

Better is a dinner of herbs where love is,
Than a fatted calf with hatred (15:17).

Solomon learned that love is the cohesive force
that binds one soul to another. It unites God
with the righteous, husband with wife, parent
with child, and friend with friend. Love is all
forgiving but must not be concealed, kept
secret.

Love must be directed toward both persons and
principles. Love is commanded for what is
right, such as wisdom, instruction, reproof,
righteousness, and purity, but one should never
love what is evil.

Love is manifested through mercy, forgiveness,
and giving. Mercy bestows loving benefits upon
its recipients, thus honoring God and bringing
favor from men. Mercy preserves rulers and is
the perfecting ingredient of good plans. It
should be extended even to animals. Such loving
mercy is rewarded by God. Forgiveness is a
form of love that restores one person to

another; it restores sinners to God and reunites friends. Giving manifests love when people help one another. Givers are able to make others welcome, attract friends, and sometimes assuage anger. Giving should follow wise principles: it should be generous, willing, impartial, and honest. It is wise to give both to God and man. In these ways, wise men attempt to love as God loves.

Love Unites Persons

God and the Righteous

The way of the wicked is an abomination to the
  LORD,
But He loves him who follows righteousness
  (15:9).

For whom the LORD loves He corrects,
Just as a father the son in whom he delights
  (3:12).

Husband and Wife

As a loving deer and a graceful doe,
Let her breasts satisfy you at all times;
And always be enraptured with her love (5:19).

Parent and Child

He who spares his rod hates his son,
But he who loves him disciplines him promptly
  (13:24).

Friends

A friend loves at all times,
And a brother is born for adversity (17:17).

Love Is Forgiving

Hatred stirs up strife,
But love covers all sins (10:12).

He who covers a transgression seeks love,
But he who repeats a matter separates the best
    of friends (17:9).

Love Must Not Be Concealed

Open rebuke is better
Than love carefully concealed (27:5).

Love What Is Right

Love Wisdom

"Get wisdom! Get understanding!
Do not forget, nor turn away from the words of
    my mouth.
Do not forsake her, and she will preserve you;
Love her, and she will keep you" (4:5–6).

"I, wisdom, dwell with prudence
And find out knowledge and discretion.
That I may cause those who love me to inherit
    wealth,
That I may fill their treasuries.
But he who sins against me wrongs his own
    soul;

All those who hate me love death" (8:12, 36).

He who gets wisdom loves his own soul;
He who keeps understanding will find good
  (19:8).

Whoever loves wisdom makes his father rejoice,
But a companion of harlots wastes his wealth
  (29:3).

Love Instruction, Reproof
Whoever loves instruction loves knowledge,
But he who hates reproof is stupid (12:1).

Do not reprove a scoffer, lest he hate you;
Rebuke a wise man, and he will love you (9:8).

A scoffer does not love one who reproves him,
Nor will he go to the wise (15:12).

Love Righteousness
Righteous lips are the delight of kings,
And they love him who speaks what is right
  (16:13).

Death and life are in the power of the tongue,
And those who love it will eat its fruit (18:21).

Love Purity
He who loves purity of heart
And has grace on his lips,
The king will be his friend (22:11).

Do Not Love What Is Wrong

Do not love sleep, lest you come to poverty;
Open your eyes, and you will be satisfied with
  bread (20:13).

He who loves pleasure will be a poor man;
He who loves wine and oil will not be rich
  (21:17).

Mercy Benefits Persons

The merciful man does good for his own soul,
But he who is cruel troubles his own flesh
  (11:17).

He who despises his neighbor sins;
But he who has mercy on the poor, happy is he
  (14:21).

It Honors God

He who oppresses the poor reproaches His
  maker,
But he who honors Him has mercy on the
  needy (14:31).

It Brings Favor

Let not mercy and truth forsake you;
Bind them around your neck,
Write them on the tablet of your heart,
And so find favor and high esteem in the sight
  of God and man (3:3-4).

He who follows righteousness and mercy
Finds life, righteousness and honor (21:21).

It Preserves Rulers

Mercy and truth preserve the king,
And by lovingkindness he upholds his throne
(20:28).

It Strengthens Plans

Do they not go astray who devise evil?
But mercy and truth belong to those who devise
good (14:22).

It Benefits Even Animals

A righteous man regards the life of his animal,
But the tender mercies of the wicked are cruel
(12:10).

God Rewards Mercy

He who has pity on the poor lends to the LORD,
And He will pay back what he has given
(19:17).

Whoever shuts his ears to the cry of the poor
Will also cry himself and not be heard (21:13).

Deliver those who are drawn toward death,
And hold back those stumbling to the slaughter.
If you say, "Surely we did not know this,"
Does not He who weighs the hearts consider it?
He who keeps your soul, does He not know it?
And will He not render to each man according
to his deeds? (24:11–12).

Forgiveness Restores

The discretion of a man makes him slow to
  anger,
And it is to his glory to overlook a transgression
  (19:11).

God and Sinners

In mercy and truth atonement is provided for
  iniquity;
And by the fear of the LORD one departs from
  evil (16:6).

He who covers his sins will not prosper,
But whoever confesses and forsakes them will
  have mercy (28:13).

Friends

He who covers a transgression seeks love,
But he who repeats a matter separates the best
  of friends (17:9).

Because of Love

Treasures of wickedness profit nothing,
But righteousness delivers from death (10:2).

Giving Helps

He who has pity on the poor lends to the LORD,
And He will pay back what he has given
  (19:17).

Giving Is Beneficial

He who has a bountiful eye will be blessed,
For he gives of his bread to the poor (22:9).

He who gives to the poor will not lack,
But he who hides his eyes will have many curses
     (28:27).

A present is a precious stone in the eyes of its
     possessor;
Wherever he turns, he prospers (17:8).

It Makes One Welcome

A man's gift makes room for him,
And brings him before great men (18:16).

It Attracts Friends

Many entreat the favor of the nobility,
And every man is a friend to one who gives
     gifts (19:6).

It Assuages Anger

A gift in secret pacifies anger,
And a bribe behind the back, strong wrath
     (21:14).

But Not Always

For jealousy is a husband's fury;
Therefore he will not spare in the day of
     vengeance.
He will accept no recompense,
Nor will he be appeased though you give many
     gifts (6:34–35).

Give Wisely

He who oppresses the poor to increase his
riches,
And he who gives to the rich, will surely come
to poverty (22:16).

Give Generously

The desire of the slothful kills him,
For his hands refuse to labor.
He covets greedily all day long,
But the righteous gives and does not spare
(21:25–26).

There is one who scatters, yet increases more;
And there is one who withholds more than is
right,
But it leads to poverty.
The generous soul will be made rich,
And he who waters will also be watered
himself.
The people will curse him who withholds grain,
But blessing will be on the head of him who
sells it (11:24–26).

There is one who makes himself rich, yet has
nothing;
And one who makes himself poor, yet has great
riches (13:7).

Give Willingly

Do not withhold good from those to whom it is
due,

When it is in the power of your hand to do so.
Do not say to your neighbor,
"Go, and come back,
And tomorrow I will give it,"
When you have it with you (3:27–28).

Do not eat the bread of a miser,
Nor desire his delicacies;
For as he thinks in his heart, so is he.
"Eat and drink!" He says to you,
But his heart is not with you.
The morsel you have eaten, you will vomit up,
And waste your pleasant words (23:6–8).

Give Impartially

If your enemy is hungry, give him bread to eat;
And if he is thirsty, give him water to drink
    (25:21).

Give Honestly

Whoever falsely boasts of giving
Is like clouds and wind without rain (25:14).

He who is greedy for gain troubles his own
    house,
But he who hates bribes will live (15:27).

A wicked man accepts a bribe behind the back
    to pervert the ways of justice (17:23).

The king establishes the land by justice,
But he who receives bribes overthrows it (29:4).

Giving to God Is Wise

Honor the LORD with your possessions,
And with the firstfruits of all your increase;
So your barns will be filled with plenty,
And your vats will overflow with new wine
    (3:9–10).

=20=

The Way of Righteousness Is Life

The way of the wicked is an abomination
  to the LORD,
But He loves him who follows righteousness (15:9).

Solomon regarded righteousness as the natural
result of wisdom; it is more excellent than
riches or ritual. It delivers from death and
brings many benefits, such as happiness, joy,
courage, peace, stability, security, satisfaction,
glory, honor, reward, life, and good government. Wise men strive to develop righteous
lives, but fools despise righteousness to their
destruction.

Righteousness Is Wisdom
A wise man fears and departs from evil,
But a fool rages and is self-confident (14:16).

Righteousness Is More Excellent

Than Riches

Better is a little with righteousness,
Than vast revenues without justice (16:8).

Than Ritual

To do righteousness and justice
Is more acceptable to the LORD than sacrifice
(21:3).

Righteousness Delivers from Death

Treasures of wickedness profit nothing,
But righteousness delivers from death.
The LORD will not allow the righteous soul to
famish,
But He casts away the desire of the wicked
(10:2–3).

Riches do not profit in the day of wrath,
But righteousness delivers from death.
The righteousness of the blameless will direct
his way aright,
But the wicked will fall by his own wickedness.
The righteousness of the upright will deliver
them,
But the unfaithful will be taken by their own
lust (11:4–6).

A man who wanders from the way of
understanding
Will rest in the congregation of the dead
(21:16).

Righteousness Brings Blessings

Blessings are on the head of the righteous,
But violence covers the mouth of the wicked.
The memory of the righteous is blessed,
But the name of the wicked will rot (10:6–7).

Happiness

Happy is the man who is always reverent,
But he who hardens his heart will fall into
  calamity (28:14).

Joy

The light of the righteous rejoices,
But the lamp of the wicked will be put out
  (13:9).

Courage

The wicked flee when no one pursues,
But the righteous are bold as a lion (28:1).

Peace

When a man's ways please the LORD,
He makes even his enemies to be at peace with
  him (16:7).

Stability

The righteous will never be removed,
But the wicked will not inhabit the earth
  (10:30).

A man is not established by wickedness,
But the root of the righteous cannot be moved
  (12:3).

The wicked are overthrown and are no more,
But the house of the righteous will stand (12:7).

Security

A righteous man hates lying,
But a wicked man is loathsome and comes to
    shame.
Righteousness keeps him whose way is
    blameless,
But wickedness overthrows the sinner (13:5–6).

The highway of the upright is to depart from
    evil;
He who keeps his way preserves his soul
    (16:17).

Satisfaction

The righteous eats to the satisfying of his soul,
But the stomach of the wicked shall be in want
    (13:25).

Glory and Honor

The silver-haired head is a crown of glory,
If it is found in the way of righteousness
    (16:31).

He who follows righteousness and mercy
Finds life, righteousness and honor (21:21).

Reward

The wicked man does deceptive work,
But to him who sows righteousness will be a
    sure reward (11:18).

Life

As righteousness leads to life,
So he who pursues evil pursues it to his own
    death (11:19).

The fruit of the righteous is a tree of life,
And he who wins souls is wise (11:30).

In the way of righteousness is life,
And in its pathway there is no death (12:28).

Good Government

Righteousness exalts a nation,
But sin is a reproach to any people (14:34).

It is an abomination for kings to commit
    wickedness,
For a throne is established by righteousness.
Righteous lips are the delight of kings,
And they love him who speaks what is right
    (16:12–13).

Take away the wicked from before the king,
And his throne will be established in
    righteousness (25:5).

Who Can Find a Faithful Man?

A faithful man will abound with
  blessings,
But he who hastens to be rich will
  not go unpunished (28:20).

Solomon found that faithfulness, integrity, and
trust are companion virtues found in the wise.
Faithfulness blesses one's health and refreshes
one's soul and is even desirable in the form of a
friend's correction. However, unfaithfulness is
destructive by its very nature. It leads to lust
and feeds on violence; it frustrates present confidence and future expectation. It is the unfortu-
nate failing of fools. Integrity is a virtue of
lasting value. It serves as a reliable guiding principle of life and maps a secure path for the wise
to follow. Trust in God is the wise way to receive divine guidance. It provides for present
happiness and future prosperity; it enables the
wise man to feel safe in the presence of impend-
ing peril, and it frees him from trusting in
riches.

The lack of these vital virtues is folly, for it

leads to contempt through resulting wickedness and poverty. Indeed, it may lead to contempt even through overabundance. Wise men cultivate faithfulness, integrity, and trust as virtues that honor God.

Faithfulness Is a Rare Virtue

Most men will proclaim each his own goodness,
But who can find a faithful man? (20:6).

Accompanies Truthfulness
A faithful witness does not lie,
But a false witness will utter lies (14:5).

Accompanies Trustworthiness
A talebearer reveals secrets,
But he who is of a faithful spirit conceals a
  matter (11:13).

Brings Health
A wicked messenger falls into trouble,
But a faithful ambassador brings health (13:17).

Refreshes One's Soul
Like the cold of snow in time of harvest
Is a faithful messenger to those who send him,
For he refreshes the soul of his masters (25:13).

Brings Friendly Correction
Faithful are the wounds of a friend,
But the kisses of an enemy are deceitful (27:6).

Unfaithfulness Destroys

The integrity of the upright will guide them,
But the perversity of the unfaithful will destroy
    them (11:3).

Good understanding gains favor,
But the way of the unfaithful is hard (13:15).

The eyes of the LORD preserve knowledge,
But He overthrows the words of the faithless
    (22:12).

Leads to Lust

The righteousness of the upright will deliver
    them,
But the unfaithful will be taken by their own
    lust (11:6).

Feeds on Violence

A man shall eat well by the fruit of his mouth,
But the soul of the unfaithful feeds on violence
    (13:2).

Frustrates Confidence

Confidence in an unfaithful man in time of
    trouble
Is like a bad tooth and a foot out of joint
    (25:19).

He who sends a message by the hand of a fool
Cuts off his own feet and drinks violence (26:6).

Frustrates Expectation

The wicked shall be a ransom for the righteous,
And the unfaithful for the upright (21:18).

Integrity Has Lasting Value

The righteous man walks in his integrity;
His children are blessed after him (20:7).

Better is the poor who walks in his integrity
Than one perverse in his ways, though he be
  rich (28:6).

Better is the poor who walks in his integrity
Than one who is perverse in his lips, and is a
  fool (19:1).

Provides Guidance

The integrity of the upright will guide them,
But the perversity of the unfaithful will destroy
  them (11:3).

Provides Security

He who walks with integrity walks securely,
But he who perverts his ways will become
  known (10:9).

Trust in God Is Wise

Incline your ear and hear the words of the wise,
And apply your heart to my knowledge;
For it is a pleasant thing if you keep them
  within you;
Let them all be fixed upon your lips,

So that your trust may be in the LORD;
I have instructed you today, even you
  (22:17–19).

Provides Guidance

Trust in the LORD with all your heart,
And lean not on your own understanding;
In all your ways acknowledge Him,
And He shall direct your paths (3:5–6).

Provides Happiness

He who heeds the word wisely will find good,
And whoever trusts in the LORD, happy is he
  (16:20).

Provides Prosperity

He who is of a proud heart stirs up strife,
But he who trusts in the LORD will be prospered
  (28:25).

Provides Safety

The fear of man brings a snare,
But whoever trusts in the LORD shall be safe
  (29:25).

Every word of God is pure;
He is a shield to those who put their trust in
  Him (30:5).

Trust in Riches Is Foolish

He who trusts in his riches will fall.
But the righteous will flourish like foliage
  (11:28).

Folly Causes Contempt

Through Wickedness

When the wicked comes, contempt comes also;
And with dishonor comes reproach (18:3).

Through Poverty

The poor man is hated even by his own
  neighbor,
But the rich has many friends.
He who despises his neighbor sins;
But he who has mercy on the poor, happy is he
  (14:20–21).

Through Overabundance

A satisfied soul loathes the honeycomb,
But to a hungry soul every bitter thing is sweet
  (27:7).

Have you found honey?
Eat only as much as you need,
Lest you be filled with it and vomit (25:16).

═22═

Seek Truth

He who speaks truth declares
  righteousness,
But a false witness, deceit (12:17).

Solomon determined that truthfulness is a righteous trait that characterizes the wise. A truthful person finds favor and esteem from both God and man. Truthfulness will deliver the innocent and find forgiveness for the guilty. It leads to permanence in the future and is the preserving ingredient of good government. However, because of the complexities of life, witnesses may require careful cross-examination before truthfulness is definitely determined.

On the other hand, untruthfulness is the height of folly. It is hated by both God and man. It leads to injustice, destruction, punishment, and death. It is the downfall of rulers and is more disgraceful than poverty. Untruthfulness is the characteristic of fools; it provides the alibis of thieves, the devices of the wicked, the delusions of the boastful, and the disguises of the hateful.

Flattery is a devious form of deception that results in the ruin of those who believe it. It sets a trap for the unsuspecting and is the worst form of rebuke. Flattery is the device of the seductress and the probe of the talebearer. Truthfulness is manifested in the standard weights and measures of the honest businessman. God delights in such honest standards, and He abhors all forms of dishonesty. He diminishes the dishonest gain of fools but prospers the wisdom of truth and honesty.

Truthfulness Is Righteous

Do they not go astray who devise evil?
But mercy and truth belong to those who devise
   good (14:22).

Truthfulness Is Wise

Does not wisdom cry out,
And understanding lift up her voice?
Listen, for I will speak of excellent things,
And from the opening of my lips will come
   right things;
For my mouth will speak truth;
Wickedness is an abomination to my lips (8:1,
   6–7).

Incline your ear and hear the words of the wise,
And apply your heart to my knowledge;
For it is a pleasant thing if you keep them
   within you;

Let them all be fixed upon your lips.
That I may make you know the certainty of the
    words of truth,
That you may answer words of truth to those
    who send to you (22:17–18; 21).

Truthfulness Leads to Favor and Esteem
Let not mercy and truth forsake you;
Bind them around your neck,
Write them on the tablet of your heart,
And so find favor and high esteem in the sight
    of God and man (3:3–4).

He who gives a right answer kisses the lips
    (24:26).

To Deliverance
A true witness delivers souls,
But a deceitful witness speaks lies (14:25).

To Forgiveness
In mercy and truth atonement is provided for
    iniquity;
And by the fear of the LORD one departs from
    evil (16:6).

To Permanence
The truthful lip shall be established forever,
But a lying tongue is but for a moment (12:19).

Preserves Good Government

Mercy and truth preserve the king,
And by lovingkindness he upholds his throne
    (20:28).

The king who judges the poor with truth,
His throne will be established forever (29:14).

Determined by Cross-Examination

The first one to plead his cause seems right,
Until his neighbor comes and examines him
    (18:17).

Untruthfulness Is Folly

Two things I request of You
(Deprive me not before I die):
Remove falsehood and lies far from me;
Give me neither poverty nor riches—
Feed me with the food You prescribe for me
    (30:7–8).

Bread gained by deceit is sweet to a man,
But afterward his mouth will be filled with
    gravel (20:17).

Untruthfulness Is Hated by God

These six things the LORD hates,
Yes, seven are an abomination to Him:
A proud look,
A lying tongue,
Hands that shed innocent blood,
A heart that devises wicked plans,

Feet that are swift in running to evil,
A false witness who speaks lies,
And one who sows discord among brethren
    (6:16–19).

Lying lips are an abomination to the LORD,
But those who deal truthfully are His delight
    (12:22).

Hated by Men
A righteous man hates lying,
But a wicked man is loathsome and comes to
    shame (13:5).

A faithful witness does not lie,
But a false witness will utter lies (14:5).

Leads to Injustice
A disreputable witness scorns justice,
And the mouth of the wicked devours iniquity
    (19:28).

Leads to Destruction
A man who bears false witness against his
    neighbor,
Is like a club, a sword, and a sharp arrow
    (25:18).

Like a madman who throws
Firebrands, arrows, and death,
Is the man who deceives his neighbor,
And says, "I was only joking!" (26:18–19).

Leads to Death

Getting treasures by a lying tongue
Is the fleeting fantasy of those who seek death
    (21:6).

Leads to Punishment

A false witness will not go unpunished,
And he who speaks lies will not escape.
A false witness will not go unpunished,
And he who speaks lies shall perish (19:5, 9).

A false witness shall perish,
But the man who hears him will speak endlessly
    (21:28).

Destroys Government

If a ruler pays attention to lies,
All his servants become wicked (29:12).

Is Worse than Poverty

What is desired in a man is kindness,
And a poor man is better than a liar (19:22).

Untruthfulness Characterizes Fools

The wisdom of the prudent is to understand his
    way,
But the folly of fools is deceit (14:8).

Thieves

Whoever is a partner with a thief hates his own
    life;
He swears to tell the truth, but reveals nothing
    (29:24).

The Wicked

The wicked man does deceptive work,
But to him who sows righteousness will be a
  sure reward (11:18).

An evildoer gives heed to false lips;
A liar listens eagerly to a spiteful tongue (17:4).

He who has a deceitful heart finds no good,
And he who has a perverse tongue falls into evil
  (17:20).

Deceit is in the heart of those who devise evil,
But counselors of peace have joy.
No grave trouble will overtake the righteous,
But the wicked shall be filled with evil
  (12:20–21).

Boasters

Whoever falsely boasts of giving
Is like clouds and wind without rain (25:14).

Haters

He who hates, disguises it with his lips,
And lays up deceit within himself;
When he speaks kindly, do not believe him,
For there are seven abominations in his heart;
Though his hatred is covered by deceit,
His wickedness will be revealed before the
  whole congregation.

A lying tongue hates those who are crushed by
   it,
And a flattering mouth works ruin (26:24–26;
   28).

Flattery Is a Curse
He who blesses his friend with a loud voice,
Rising early in the morning,
It will be counted a curse to him (27:14).

Works Ruin
A lying tongue hates those who are crushed by
   it,
And a flattering mouth works ruin (26:28).

Sets a Trap
A man who flatters his neighbor
Spreads a net for his feet (29:5).

Worse Than Rebuke
He who rebukes a man will find more favor
   afterward
Than he who flatters with the tongue (28:23).

Practiced by Seductresses
To deliver you from the immoral woman,
From the seductress who flatters with her words
   (2:16).

To keep you from the evil woman,
From the flattering tongue of a seductress (6:24).

That they may keep you from the immoral
    woman,
From the seductress who flatters with her
    words.
With her enticing speech she caused him to
    yield,
With her flattering lips she seduced him (7:5,
    21).

Practiced by Talebearers
He who goes about as a talebearer reveals
    secrets;
Therefore do not associate with one who flatters
    with his lips (20:19).

God Delights in Honest Standards
A false balance is an abomination to the LORD,
But a just weight is His delight (11:1).

A just weight and balance are the LORD'S;
All the weights in the bag are His work (16:11).

God Abhors Dishonest Standards
Diverse weights and diverse measures,
They are both alike, an abomination to the
    LORD (20:10).

Diverse weights are an abomination to the
    LORD,
And a false balance is not good (20:23).

Do not remove the ancient landmark
Which your fathers have set (22:28).

Dishonest Gain Diminishes

"It is good for nothing," cries the buyer;
But when he has gone his way, then he boasts
(20:14).

Wealth gained by dishonesty will be diminished,
But he who gathers by labor will increase
(13:11).

=23=

The Tongue of the Wise

The words of a man's mouth are deep
    waters;
The wellspring of wisdom is a flowing
    brook (18:4).
A word fitly spoken is like apples of gold
    in settings of silver (25:11).

"The tongue is a little member and boasts great things" (James 3:5). Solomon portrayed human speech as a powerful instrument for either good or evil. Wise speech brings bountiful blessings to man and worshipful praise to God. Foolish speech brings curses and destruction to man and blasphemy to God. Sound speech is the righteous practice of the wise. It is not blunt and hasty but thoughtful and restrained. It is used to preserve life and provide deliverance. It is the source of satisfaction, prosperity, joy, and pleasantness.

Righteous speech is as profitable as riches. It is expected of rulers and should be honored by them, and knowledgeable speech is of like value. Pleasant speech overcomes impossible barriers; it is the tool of the teacher for the advancement of learning and the technique of the therapist for the enhancement of healing. Gentle speech has the power of persuasion but is rarely found on the lips of the rich.

Foolish speech is profitless prattle. Its hasty utterances lead to poverty and destruction. False speech broadcasts the wicked word of the unwise. It results in evil, distrust, anger, and destruction. But unfounded curses cause no harm to the one who is aware of its foolish source.

Gossip is the speech of the ungodly. It comes from unfaithful sources and tends to be unending. It uses flattery to uncover secrets with which to ruin friendships. It perpetuates strife and contaminates the soul of the talebearer. Even when given with no evil intent, gossip often has ruinous repercussions. In contrast, the wise man deliberately uses his gift of speech to bring good to mankind and glory to God.

Sound Speech Is Righteous
He who speaks truth declares righteousness,
But a false witness, deceit (12:17).

It is Wise
Wisdom is found on the lips of him who has
    understanding,
But a rod is for the back of him who is devoid
    of understanding (10:13).

The mouth of the righteous brings forth
  wisdom,
But the perverse tongue will be cut out.
The lips of the righteous know what is
  acceptable,
But the mouth of the wicked what is perverse
  (10:31–32).

The tongue of the wise uses knowledge rightly,
But the mouth of fools pours forth foolishness
  (15:2).

The lips of the wise disperse knowledge,
But the heart of the fool does not do so (15:7).

The heart of the wise teaches his mouth,
And adds learning to his lips (16:23).

Excellent speech is not becoming to a fool,
Much less lying lips to a prince (17:7).

It Is Thoughtful

The heart of the righteous studies how to
  answer,
But the mouth of the wicked pours forth evil
  (15:28).

It Is Restrained

In the multitude of words sin is not lacking,
But he who restrains his lips is wise (10:19).

He who is devoid of wisdom despises his
  neighbor,

But a man of understanding holds his peace
(11:12).

Wisdom rests quietly in the heart of him who
has understanding,
But what is in the heart of fools is made known
(14:33).

Even a fool is counted wise when he holds his
peace;
When he shuts his lips, he is considered
perceptive (17:28).

A fool has no delight in understanding,
But in expressing his own heart (18:2).

Whoever guards his mouth and tongue
Keeps his soul from troubles (21:23).

Do not speak in the hearing of a fool,
For he will despise the wisdom of your words
(23:9).

A fool vents all his feelings,
But a wise man holds them back (29:11).

It Leads to Life
The mouth of the righteous is a well of life,
But violence covers the mouth of the wicked
(10:11).

He who guards his mouth preserves his life,
But he who opens wide his lips shall have
destruction (13:3).

A wholesome tongue is a tree of life,
But perverseness in it breaks the spirit (15:4).

Death and life are in the power of the tongue,
And those who love it will eat its fruit (18:21).

It Leads to Deliverance

The words of the wicked are, "Lie in wait for
blood,"
But the mouth of the upright will deliver them
(12:6).

In the mouth of a fool is a rod of pride,
But the lips of the wise will preserve them
(14:3).

A soft answer turns away wrath,
But a harsh word stirs up anger (15:1).

It Leads to Satisfaction

A man will be satisifed with good by the fruit
of his mouth,
And the recompense of a man's hands will be
rendered to him (12:14).

A man's stomach shall be satisfied from the fruit
of his mouth,
And from the produce of his lips he shall be
filled (18:20).

It Leads to Prosperity

A man shall eat well by the fruit of his mouth,
But the soul of the unfaithful feeds on violence
(13:2).

It Leads to Joy

A man has joy by the answer of his mouth,
And a word spoken in due season, how good it
    is! (15:23).

The light of the eyes rejoices the heart,
And a good report makes the bones healthy
    (15:30).

My son, if your heart is wise,
My heart will rejoice—indeed, I myself;
Yes, my inmost being will rejoice
When your lips speak right things (23:15-16).

As cold water to a weary soul,
So is good news from a far country (25:25).

Anxiety in the heart of man causes depression,
But a good word makes it glad (12:25).

It Leads to Pleasantness

The thoughts of the wicked are an abomination
    to the LORD,
But the words of the pure are pleasant (15:26).

Righteous Speech Is Profitable

The tongue of the righteous is choice silver;
The heart of the wicked is worth little.
The lips of the righteous feed many,
But fools die for lack of wisdom (10:20-21).

It Is Expected of Rulers

Even though divination is on the lips of the
    king,
His mouth must not transgress in judgment
    (16:10).

It Is Honored By Rulers

Righteous lips are the delight of kings,
And they love him who speaks what is right
    (16:13).

Knowledgeable Speech Is Valuable

There is gold and a multitude of rubies,
But the lips of knowledge are a precious jewel
    (20:15).

Incline your ear and hear the words of the wise,
And apply your heart to my knowledge;
For it is a pleasant thing if you keep them
    within you;
Let them all be fixed upon your lips,
So that your trust may be in the LORD;
I have instructed you today, even you.
Have I not written to you excellent things
Of counsels and knowledge,
That I may make you know the certainty of the
    words of truth,
That you may answer words of truth
To those who send to you? (22:17–21).

Pleasant Speech Is Helpful

It Aids Learning

The wise in heart will be called prudent,
And sweetness of the lips increases learning
  (16:21).

It Aids Health

Pleasant words are like a honeycomb,
Sweetness to the soul and health to the bones
  (16:24).

There is one who speaks like the piercings of a
  sword,
But the tongue of the wise promotes health
  (12:18).

Gentle Speech Is Powerful

It Is Persuasive

By long forbearance a ruler is persuaded,
And a gentle tongue breaks a bone (25:15).

But Not Used by the Rich

The poor man uses entreaties,
But the rich answers roughly (18:23).

Foolish Speech Is Profitless

A prudent man conceals knowledge,
But the heart of fools proclaims foolishness
  (12:23).

Go from the presence of a foolish man,
When you do not perceive in him the lips of
    knowledge (14:7).

It Is Hasty

He who answers a matter before he hears it,
It is folly and shame to him (18:13).

Do you see a man hasty in his words?
There is more hope for a fool than for him
    (29:20).

It Leads to Poverty

In all labor there is profit,
But idle chatter leads only to poverty (14:23).

It Destroys

Wise people store up knowledge,
But the mouth of the foolish is near destruction
    (10:14).

The wicked is ensnared by the transgression of
    his lips,
But the righteous will come through trouble
    (12:13).

A disreputable witness scorns justice,
And the mouth of the wicked devours iniquity
    (19:28).

The mouth of an immoral woman is a deep pit;
He who is abhorred of the LORD will fall there
    (22:14).

A fool's mouth is his destruction,

And his lips are the snare of his soul (18:7).

False Speech Is Wicked

Fervent lips with a wicked heart
Are like earthenware covered with silver dross
(26:23).

It Leads to Evil

An evildoer gives heed to false lips;
A liar listens eagerly to a spiteful tongue (17:4).

He who has a deceitful heart finds no good,
And he who has a perverse tongue falls into evil
(17:20).

It Leads to Distrust

He who hates, disguises it with his lips,
And lays up deceit within himself;
When he speaks kindly, do not believe him,
For there are seven abominations in his heart;
Though his hatred is covered by deceit,
His wickedness will be revealed before the
whole congregation (26:24-26).

It Leads to Anger

The north wind brings forth rain,
And a backbiting tongue an angry countenance
(25:23).

It Leads to Destruction

A lying tongue hates those who are crushed by
it,
And a flattering mouth works ruin (26:28).

Unfounded Curse Causes No Hurt

Like a flitting sparrow, like a flying swallow,
So a curse without cause shall not alight (26:2).

Gossip Is Ungodly

An ungodly man digs up evil,
And it is on his lips like a burning fire (16:27).

It Is Unfaithful

A talebearer reveals secrets,
But he who is of a faithful spirit conceals a
matter (11:13).

It Is Unending

A false witness shall perish,
But the man who hears him will speak endlessly
(21:28).

It Uses Flattery

He who goes about as a talebearer reveals
secrets;
Therefore do not associate with one who flatters
with his lips (20:19).

It Ruins Friendship

A perverse man sows strife,
And a whisperer separates the best of friends
(16:28).

He who covers a transgression seeks love,
But he who repeats a matter separates the best
of friends (17:9).

It Perpetuates Strife

Where there is no wood, the fire goes out;
And where there is no talebearer, strife ceases
   (26:20).

It Contaminates

The words of a talebearer are like tasty trifles,
And they go down into the inmost body (18:8;
   26:22).

It May Have Repercussions

Do not malign a servant to his master,
Lest he curse you, and you be found guilty
   (30:10).

=== 24 ===

Before Honor Is Humility

Better to be of a humble spirit with the
  lowly,
Than to divide the spoil with the proud
  (16:19).

Solomon frequently contrasted humility and pride. By exercising humility, the wise man develops a balanced self-image, neither degrading nor exalting himself. He learns that true honor comes from others and is earned through humble service. True humility retains such honor by not disappointing those from whom it comes.

Fools have no such wisdom but seek their own honor in pride. Such pride is sin and is hated by God. It stirs up such destructive forces as arrogance, shame, contention, contempt, and strife, all of which deliver dishonor to the proud fool. Only the wise recognize the sensibility of humility.

The Wise Are Humble

When pride comes, then comes shame;
But with the humble is wisdom (11:2).

Humility Precedes Honor

The fear of the LORD is the instruction of
    wisdom,
And before honor is humility (15:33).

Before destruction the heart of a man is
    haughty,
And before honor is humility (18:12).

By humility and the fear of the LORD
Are riches and honor and life (22:4).

Humility Retains Honor

A man's pride will bring him low,
But the humble in spirit will retain honor
    (29:23).

Fools Are Proud

In the mouth of a fool is a rod of pride,
But the lips of the wise will preserve them
    (14:3).

Pride Is Sin

A haughty look, a proud heart,
And the plowing of the wicked are sin (21:4).

God Hates Pride

These six things the LORD hates,
Yes, seven are an abomination to Him:
A proud look,
A lying tongue,
Hands that shed innocent blood (6:16–17).

Everyone who is proud in heart is an
    abomination to the LORD;
Though they join forces, none will go
    unpunished (16:5).

The LORD will destroy the house of the proud,
But He will establish the boundary of the
    widow (15:25).

Pride Brings Destruction

Pride goes before destruction,
And a haughty spirit before a fall (16:18).

Before destruction the heart of a man is
    haughty,
And before honor is humility (18:12).

With Arrogance

There is a generation—oh, how lofty are their
    eyes!
And their eyelids are lifted up (30:13).

With Shame

When pride comes, then comes shame;
But with the humble is wisdom (11:2).

With Contention

By pride comes only contention,
But with the well-advised is wisdom (13:10).

With Contempt

A proud and haughty man—
"Scoffer" is his name;
He acts with arrogant pride (21:24).

With Strife

He who is of a proud heart stirs up strife,
But he who trusts in the LORD will be prospered
    (28:25).

With Dishonor

A man's pride will bring him low,
But the humble in spirit will retain honor
    (29:23).

═25═

The Wise Have Self-Control

Keep your heart with all diligence,
For out of it spring the issues of life
(4:23).

Solomon observed that self-control is a mark of strength and wisdom. It is acquired through diligent efforts to gain control of the temper and to develop a moderate style of life. Self-control results in a good reputation that is far more valuable than riches but that may be ruined by deeds of injustice.

Lack of self-control is a mark of weakness and folly. It may manifest itself by such characteristics as proud self-confidence and self-esteem, by self-seeking and self-exalting attitudes. Such characteristics must be overcome, because they are destructive in nature; one would be much better off to suffer reproach than to seek his own praise.

Lack of self-control also is revealed by self-righteousness. This is a prominent trait of fools and a sign of unfaithfulness.

Self-righteousness leads to destruction because it will be judged by God. It is far better to confess and forsake it in favor of true righteousness. Wise men work diligently at developing self-control.

Self-Control Requires Diligence
Keep your heart with all diligence,
For out of it spring the issues of life.
Put away from you a deceitful mouth,
And put perverse lips far from you.
Let your eyes look straight ahead,
And your eyelids look right before you.
Ponder the path of your feet,
And let all your ways be established.
Do not turn to the right or the left;
Remove your foot from evil (4:23–27).

Demonstrated by Controlled Temper
A wrathful man stirs up strife,
But he who is slow to anger allays contention (15:18).

He who is slow to anger is better than the mighty,
And he who rules his spirit than he who takes a city (16:32).

Demonstrated by Moderation
When you sit down to eat with a ruler,
Consider carefully what is before you;

And put a knife to your throat if you are a man
   given to appetite.
Do not desire his delicacies,
For they are deceptive food (23:1-3).

Self-Control Develops Reputation

The refining pot is for silver and the furnace for
   gold,
And a man is valued by what others say of him
   (27:21).

Even a child is known by his deeds,
By whether what he does is pure and right
   (20:11).

The glory of young men is their strength,
And the splendor of old men is their gray head
   (20:29).

Which Is Better Than Riches

A good name is to be chosen rather than great
   riches,
Loving favor rather than silver and gold (22:1).

Which Is Ruined By Injustice

Do not go hastily to court;
For what will you do in the end,
When your neighbor has put you to shame?
Debate your case with your neighbor himself,
And do not disclose the secret to another;
Lest he who hears it expose your shame,
And your reputation be ruined (25:8-10).

Lack of Self-Control Is Weakness

Whoever has no rule over his own spirit
Is like a city broken down, without walls
(25:28).

Revealed By Proud Self-Confidence

A wise man fears and departs from evil,
But a fool rages and is self-confident (14:16).

He who trusts in his own heart is a fool,
But whoever walks wisely will be delivered
(28:26).

Revealed By Proud Self-Esteem

Do not be wise in your own eyes;
Fear the LORD and depart from evil.
It will be health to your flesh,
And strength to your bones (3:7–8).

Do you see a man wise in his own eyes?
There is more hope for a fool than for him
(26:12).

The rich man is wise in his own eyes,
But the poor who has understanding searches
him out (28:11).

Revealed by Self-Seeking

A man who isolates himself seeks his own
desire;
He rages against all wise judgment (18:1).

Revealed by Self-Exaltation

It is not good to eat much honey;
So to seek one's own glory is not glory (25:27).

Let another man praise you, and not your own
  mouth;
A stranger, and not your own lips (27:2).

If you have been foolish in exalting yourself,
Or if you have devised evil, put your hand on
  your mouth (30:32).

He who loves transgression loves strife,
And he who exalts his gate seeks destruction
  (17:19).

Reproach Is Preferable

Better is the one who is slighted but has a
  servant,
Than he who honors himself but lacks bread
  (12:9).

Do not exalt yourself in the presence of the
  king,
And do not stand in the place of great men;
For it is better that he say to you,
"Come up here,"
Than that you should be put lower in the
  presence of the prince,
Whom your eyes have seen (25:6–7).

Revealed by Self-Righteousness

There is a generation that curses its father,
And does not bless its mother.

There is a generation that is pure in its own
   eyes,
Yet is not washed from its filthiness (30:11–12).

Who can say, "I have made my heart clean,
I am pure from my sin"? (20:9).

The way of a fool is right in his own eyes,
But he who heeds counsel is wise (12:15).

Most men will proclaim each his own goodness,
But who can find a faithful man? (20:6).

Whoever robs his father or his mother,
And says,"It is no transgression,"
The same is companion to a destroyer (28:24).

There is a way which seems right to a man,
But its end is the way of death.
There is a way that seems right to a man,
But its end is the way of death (14:12; 16:25).

All the ways of a man are pure in his own eyes,
But the LORD weighs the spirits (16:2).

Every way of a man is right in his own eyes,
But the LORD weighs the hearts (21:2).

He who covers his sins will not prosper,
But whoever confesses and forsakes them will
   have mercy (28:13).

=26=

The Joy of Doing Justice

But the path of the just is like the shining
   sun,
That shines ever brighter unto the perfect
   day.
The way of the wicked is like darkness;
They do not know what makes them
   stumble (4:18–19).

Solomon spent forty years administering justice
to the nation of Israel. He had a practical
knowledge of what justice means to the common person. He declared that God's Word
teaches justice, that God Himself delights in it
and blesses the just person. Government must
promote justice for all citizens. The just are wise
because they receive instructions about justice
and seek the well-being of those who are blameless.

However, justice may be perverted by such unwise practices as drinking and giving bribes.
God hates injustice: it causes cruel waste and

222

undeserved punishment; it is prone to partiality and to disreputable testimony. The wicked refuse to do justice; they seem not to understand it. This brings them to ultimate punishment—the destiny of fools. Wise men seek justice for all and are committed to correcting injustice wherever it is found.

God's Word Teaches Justice

The proverbs of Solomon the son of David,
King of Israel.
To receive the instruction of wisdom,
Justice, judgment, and equity (1:1, 3).

God Delights in Justice

A false balance is an abomination to the LORD,
But a just weight is His delight (11:1).

To do righteousness and justice is more
acceptable to the LORD than sacrifice (21:3).

God Blesses the Just

The curse of the LORD is on the house of the
wicked,
But He blesses the habitation of the just (3:33).

A good man leaves an inheritance to his
children's children,
But the wealth of the sinner is stored up for the
righteous (13:22).

Government Must Promote Justice

The king establishes the land by justice,
But he who receives bribes overthrows it (29:4).

"I, wisdom, dwell with prudence,
And find out knowledge and discretion.
By me kings reign,
And rulers decree justice" (8:12, 15).

It is the glory of God to conceal a matter,
But the glory of kings is to search out a matter
    (25:2).

Open your mouth for the speechless,
In the cause of all who are appointed to die.
Open your mouth, judge righteously,
And plead the cause of the poor and needy
    (31:8–9).

The Just Are Wise

The mouth of the righteous brings forth
    wisdom,
But the perverse tongue will be cut out (10:31).

They Receive Instruction

Give instruction to a wise man, and he will be
    still wiser;
Teach a just man, and he will increase in
    learning (9:9).

They Seek Well-Being

The bloodthirsty hate the blameless,
But the just seek his well-being (29:10).

Justice May Be Perverted

By Drinking

It is not for kings, O Lemuel,
It is not for kings to drink wine,
Nor for princes intoxicating drink;
Lest they drink and forget the law,
And pervert the justice of all the afflicted
    (31:4–5).

By Bribery

A wicked man accepts a bribe behind the back
To pervert the ways of justice (17:23).

God Hates Injustice

He who justifies the wicked, and he who
    condemns the just,
Both of them alike are an abomination to the
    LORD (17:15).

An unjust man is an abomination to the
    righteous,
And he who is upright in the way is an
    abomination to the wicked (29:27).

It Causes Waste

Much food is in the fallow ground of the poor,
And for lack of justice there is waste (13:23).

It Gives Undeserved Punishment

Also, to punish the righteous is not good,
Nor to strike princes for their uprightness
    (17:26).

It Shows Partiality

It is not good to show partiality to the wicked,
Or to overthrow the righteous in judgment
  (18:5).

These things also belong to the wise:
It is not good to show partiality in judgment.
He who says to the wicked,
"You are righteous,"
Him the people will curse;
Nations will abhor him.
But those who rebuke the wicked will have
  delight,
And a good blessing will come upon them
  (24:23–25).

To show partiality is not good,
Because for a piece of bread a man will
  transgress (28:21).

It Gives Disreputable Witness

A disreputable witness scorns justice,
And the mouth of the wicked devours iniquity
  (19:28).

The Wicked Are Unjust

The violence of the wicked will destroy them,
Because they refuse to do justice (21:7).

They Do Not Understand Justice

Evil men do not understand justice,
But those who seek the LORD understand all
  (28:5).

They Will Be Punished
Though they join forces,
The wicked will not go unpunished;
But the posterity of the righteous will be
    delivered (11:21).

=27=

The Way of the Lord Is Strength

The glory of young men is their strength,
And the splendor of old men is their gray
head (20:29).

E veryone has a basic need for strength,
security, and satisfaction. Solomon knew the
characteristics of true strength. He admired it
and commended it to all. He noted that true
strength comes from God through wisdom,
although the rich tend to depend on their
wealth for strength. True strength is profitable
to the wise because it enables them to endure
adversity. However, the strong may be
destroyed if they give in to immorality or the
influence of others. The wise are strong enough
to avoid such folly.

Security is sought by all but is the sure
possession of only the righteous; wicked fools
can look forward to ultimate doom. True
security comes from God through wisdom and
counsel, though a good neighbor provides a
measure of temporal security.

Likewise satisfaction comes from above. It is the natural result of righteous living, hard work, and accomplishment. Satisfaction also comes through sound speech and a happy marriage. However, for a fool, satisfaction may lead to contempt, and some things can never be satisfied. The wise find their ultimate strength, security, and satisfaction in God.

Strength Comes from God

In the fear of the LORD there is strong confidence,
And His children will have a place of refuge (14:26).

The name of the LORD is a strong tower;
The righteous run to it and are safe (18:10).

The way of the LORD is strength for the upright,
But destruction will come to the workers of iniquity (10:29).

Strength Comes from Wisdom

"Counsel is mine, and sound wisdom;
I am understanding, I have strength" (8:14).

A wise man scales the city of the mighty,
And brings down the trusted stronghold (21:22).

A wise man is strong,
Yes, a man of knowledge increases strength (24:5).

Strength Comes from Wealth

The rich man's wealth is his strong city;
The destruction of the poor is their poverty
    (10:15).

The rich man's wealth is his strong city,
And like a high wall in his own esteem (18:11).

Strength Provides Profit

Where no oxen are, the trough is clean;
But much increase comes by the strength of an
    ox (14:4).

Strength Endures Adversity

If you faint in the day of adversity,
Your strength is small (24:10).

Strength May Be Destroyed

By External Influence
What, my son?
And what, son of my womb?
And what, son of my vows?
Do not give your strength to women,
Nor your ways to that which destroys kings
    (31:2–3).

By Immorality
And there a woman met him,
With the attire of a harlot, and a crafty heart.
With her enticing speech she caused him to
    yield,

With her flattering lips she seduced him.
For she has cast down many wounded,
And all who were slain by her were strong men
    (7:10, 21, 26).

The Righteous Have Security

When the whirlwind passes by, the wicked is no
    more,
But the righteous has an everlasting foundation
    (10:25).

The highway of the upright is to depart from
    evil;
He who keeps his way preserves his soul
    (16:17).

A wicked man hardens his face,
But as for the upright, he establishes his way
    (21:29).

It Comes from the Lord

The name of the LORD is a strong tower;
The righteous run to it and are safe (18:10).

The fear of man brings a snare,
But whoever trusts in the LORD shall be safe
    (29:25).

It Comes from Wisdom

Wisdom calls aloud outside;
She raises her voice in the open squares.
"But whoever listens to me will dwell safely,

And will be secure, without fear of evil "(1:20, 33).

My son, let them not depart from your eyes—
Keep sound wisdom and discretion;
So they will be life to your soul and grace to
    your neck.
Then you will walk safely in your way,
And your foot will not stumble.
When you lie down, you will not be afraid;
Yes, you will lie down and your sleep will be
    sweet.
Do not be afraid of sudden terror,
Nor of trouble from the wicked when it comes;
For the LORD will be your confidence,
And will keep your foot from being caught
    (3:21–26).

There are four things which are little on the
    earth,
But they are exceedingly wise.
The rock badgers are a feeble folk,
Yet they make their homes in the crags (30:24,
    26).

It Comes from Counsel
Where there is no counsel, the people fall;
But in the multitude of counselors there is
    safety (11:14).

For by wise counsel you will wage your own
    war,

And in a multitude of counselors there is safety
(24:6).

It Comes from Good Neighbors
Do not devise evil against your neighbor,
For he dwells by you for safety's sake (3:29).

Satisfaction Is from Above
The backslider in heart will be filled with his
own ways,
But a good man will be satisfied from above
(14:14).

Through Righteousness
The righteous eats to the satisfying of his soul,
But the stomach of the wicked shall be in want
(13:25).

The fear of the LORD leads to life,
And he who has it will abide in satisfaction;
He will not be visited with evil (19:23).

Through Hard Work
He who tills his land will be satisfied with
bread,
But he who follows frivolity is devoid of
understanding (12:11).

Do not love sleep, lest you come to poverty;
Open your eyes, and you will be satisfied with
bread (20:13).

Through Accomplishment

A desire accomplished is sweet to the soul,
But it is an abomination to fools to depart from
    evil (13:19).

Through Sound Speech

The wicked is ensnared by the transgression of
    his lips,
But the righteous will come through trouble.
A man will be satisifed with good by the fruit
    of his mouth,
And the recompense of a man's hands will be
    rendered to him (12:13–14).

A man's stomach shall be satisfied from the fruit
    of his mouth,
And from the produce of his lips he shall be
    filled (18:20).

Through Happy Marriage

Drink water from your own cistern,
And running water from your own well.
Should your fountains be dispersed abroad,
Streams of water in the streets?
Let them be only your own,
And not for strangers with you.
Let your fountain be blessed,
And rejoice with the wife of your youth.
As a loving deer and a graceful doe,
Let her breasts satisfy you at all times;
And always be enraptured with her love.
For why should you, my son,

Be enraptured by an immoral woman,
And be embraced in the arms of a seductress?
   (5:15–20).

Satisfaction May Lead to Contempt
A satisfied soul loathes the honeycomb,
But to a hungry soul every bitter thing is sweet
   (27:7).

Some Things Are Never Satisfied
Hell and Destruction are never full;
So the eyes of man are never satisfied (27:20).

The leech has two daughters,
Crying, "Give! Give!"
There are three things that are never satisfied,
Four things never say, "It is enough":
The grave, the barren womb,
The earth that is not satisfied with water,
And the fire that never says, "It is enough."
   (30:15–16).

=28=

The Way of Life Winds Upward

The fear of the LORD leads to life,
And he who has it will abide in
    satisfaction;
He will not be visited with evil (19:23).

Life, longevity, and old age were often on Solomon's mind. He experienced life's fullness and gave advice on how others could achieve it. His road map to life begins with the paths of righteousness, traverses the ways of wisdom, explores the avenues of instruction and understanding, and travels in the direction of hope. The wayside stops are at the auditorium of sound speech, the college of God's Word, and the temple of worship. The highway displays road signs warning of wicked threats to life, such as theft, greed, immorality, and foolish talk.

The highway moves on to the destination of long life, continuing the route of wisdom and instruction, through the land of contentment over the broadway of obedience. At last the

glorious goal of old age is gained at the gateway
of eternity.

Paths of Righteousness Lead to Life

In the way of righteousness is life,
And in its pathway there is no death (12:28).

The mouth of the righteous is a well of life,
But violence covers the mouth of the wicked
(10:11).

The labor of the righteous leads to life,
The wages of the wicked to sin (10:16).

The fruit of the righteous is a tree of life,
And he who wins souls is wise (11:30).

A sound heart is life to the body,
But envy is rottenness to the bones (14:30).

The way of life winds upward for the wise,
That he may turn away from hell below (15:24).

Every way of a man is right in his own eyes,
But the LORD weighs the hearts (21:2).

The Path of Wisdom

Happy is the man who finds wisdom,
And the man who gains understanding;
For her proceeds are better than the profits of
silver,
And her gain than fine gold.
She is a tree of life to those who take hold of
her,

And happy are all who retain her (3:13–14; 18).

My son, let them not depart from your eyes—
Keep sound wisdom and discretion;
So they will be life to your soul and grace to
    your neck (3:21–22).

"For whoever finds me finds life,
And obtains favor from the LORD" (8:35).

The law of the wise is a fountain of life,
To turn one away from the snares of death
    (13:14).

The Path of Instruction

My son, give attention to my words;
Incline your ear to my sayings.
Do not let them depart from your eyes;
Keep them in the midst of your heart;
For they are life to those who find them,
And health to all their flesh.
Keep your heart with all diligence,
For out of it spring the issues of life (4:20–23).

He who keeps instruction is in the way of life,
But he who refuses reproof goes astray (10:17).

The ear that hears the reproof of life
Will abide among the wise (15:31).

The Path of Understanding

Understanding is a wellspring of life to him who
    has it.
But the correction of fools is folly (16:22).

The Path of Hope

Hope deferred makes the heart sick,
But when the desire comes, it is a tree of life
(13:12).

The Path of Wholesome Speech

A wholesome tongue is a tree of life,
But perverseness in it breaks the spirit (15:4).

Death and life are in the power of the tongue,
And those who love it will eat its fruit (18:21).

The Word of God

For the commandment is a lamp, and the law is
light;
Reproofs of instruction are the way of life,
(6:23).

The Fear of the Lord

The fear of the LORD is a fountain of life,
To avoid the snares of death (14:27).

The fear of the LORD leads to life,
And he who has it will abide in satisfaction;
He will not be visited with evil (19:23).

By humility and the fear of the LORD
Are riches and honor and life (22:4).

Riches Ransom a Man's Life

The ransom of a man's life is his riches,
But the poor does not hear rebuke (13:8).

Wickedness Threatens Life

As righteousness leads to life,
So he who pursues evil pursues it to his own
   death (11:19).

By Theft

Whoever is a partner with a thief hates his own
   life;
He swears to tell the truth, but reveals nothing
   (29:24).

By Greed

So are the ways of everyone who is greedy for
   gain;
It takes away the life of its owners (1:19).

By Immorality

To deliver you from the immoral woman,
From the seductress who flatters with her
   words,
Who forsakes the companion of her youth,
And forgets the covenant of her God.
For her house leads down to death,
And her paths to the dead;
None who go to her return,
Nor do they regain the paths of life (2:16–19).

For the lips of an immoral woman drip honey,
And her mouth is smoother than oil;
But in the end she is bitter as wormwood,
Sharp as a two-edged sword.
Her feet go down to death.
Her steps lay hold of hell.

Lest you ponder her path of life—
Her ways are unstable;
You do not know them (5:3–6).

For by means of a harlot a man is reduced to a
    crust of bread;
And an adulteress will prey upon his precious
    life (6:26).

With her enticing speech she caused him to
    yield,
With her flattering lips she seduced him.
Immediately he went after her,
As an ox goes to the slaughter,
Or as a fool to the correction of the stocks,
Till an arrow struck his liver.
As a bird hastens to the snare,
He did not know it would take his life
    (7:21–23).

By Foolish Talk
He who guards his mouth preserves his life,
But he who opens wide his lips shall have
    destruction (13:3).

Righteous Paths Lead to Long Life
The fear of the LORD prolongs days,
But the years of the wicked will be shortened
    (10:27).

The Path of Wisdom

Happy is the man who finds wisdom,
And the man who gains understanding;
For her proceeds are better than the profits of
    silver,
And her gain than fine gold.
Length of days is in her right hand,
In her left hand riches and honor (3:13–14, 16).

For by me your days will be multiplied,
And years of life will be added to you (9:11).

The Path of Instruction

My son, do not forget my law,
But let your heart keep my commands;
For length of days and long life
And peace they will add to you (3:1–2).

Hear, my son, and receive my sayings,
And the years of your life will be many (4:10).

Train up a child in the way he should go,
And when he is old he will not depart from it
    (22:6)

The Path of Contentment

A ruler who lacks understanding is a great
    oppressor,
But he who hates covetousness will prolong his
    days (28:16).

The Path of Obedience

Listen to counsel and receive instruction,
That you may be wise in your latter days
     (19:20).

Old Age Has Its Glory

Children's children are the crown of old men,
And the glory of children is their father (17:6).

The silver-haired head is a crown of glory,
If it is found in the way of righteousness
     (16:31).

The glory of young men is their strength,
And the splendor of old men is their gray head
     (20:29).

Listen to your father who begot you,
And do not despise your mother when she is
     old (23:22).

=29=

The Hope of the Righteous

> Do not let your heart envy sinners,
> But in the fear of the LORD continue all
>   day long;
> For surely there is a hereafter,
> And your hope will not be cut off (23:17–
>   18).

Hope is the expectation of good results or a
blessed hereafter. Solomon spoke of the sure
hope of the righteous and the wise and of the
hopeful results of chastening. Accomplished
hope brings great satisfaction, but deferred hope
brings discouragement.

The wicked have little for which to hope. Their
hopeful plans perish; their deepest fears come
upon them, and they reap the results of their
wrongful ways. Their hope deteriorates into
humiliation, doom, darkness, and wrath.
Indeed, there are some who have no hope at all:
the fool is hopelessly filled with folly; the man
of great wrath is hopelessly doomed to
punishment; the impetuous man is hopelessly
destined to failure; and the conceited man is

hopelessly committed to vanity. Wise men hope
in the sure promises of God's Word.

The Righteous Have a Sure Hope

The fear of the LORD prolongs days,
But the years of the wicked will be shortened.
The hope of the righteous will be gladness,
But the expectation of the wicked will perish
   (10:27–28).

The wicked is banished in his wickedness,
But the righteous has a refuge in his death
   (14:32).

The Wise Have a Sure Hope

The way of life winds upward for the wise,
That he may turn away from hell below (15:24).

My son, eat honey because it is good,
And the honeycomb which is sweet to your
   taste;
So shall the knowledge of wisdom be to your
   soul;
If you have found it, there is a prospect,
And your hope will not be cut off (24:13–14).

There Is Hope in Chastening

Chasten your son while there is hope,
And do not set your heart on his destruction
   (19:18).

Accomplished Hope Satisfies

A desire accomplished is sweet to the soul,
But it is an abomination to fools to depart from
  evil (13:19).

Deferred Hope Discourages

Hope deferred makes the heart sick,
But when the desire comes, it is a tree of life
  (13:12).

The Hope of the Wicked Perishes

When a wicked man dies, his expectation will
  perish,
And the hope of the unjust perishes.
The righteous is delivered from trouble,
And it comes to the wicked instead (11:7–8).

The house of the wicked will be overthrown,
But the tent of the upright will flourish (14:11).

Their Deepest Fears Happen

The fear of the wicked will come upon him,
And the desire of the righteous will be granted.
When the whirlwind passes by, the wicked is no
  more,
But the righteous has an everlasting foundation
  (10:24–25).

They Reap Their Own Ways

The backslider in heart will be filled with his
  own ways,

But a good man will be satisfied from above
 (14:14).

The Wicked Are Humbled

The evil will bow before the good,
And the wicked at the gates of the righteous
 (14:19).

Doomed

The LORD has made all things for Himself,
Yes, even the wicked for the day of doom
 (16:4).

In Darkness

Do not fret because of evil doers,
Nor be envious of the wicked;
For there will be no prospect for the evil man;
The lamp of the wicked will be put out
 (24:19–20).

In Wrath

The desire of the righteous is only good,
But the expectation of the wicked is wrath
 (11:23).

Some Have No Hope

He who is often reproved, and hardens his
 neck,
Will suddenly be destroyed, and that without
 remedy (29:1).

The Fool

As a dog returns to his own vomit,
So a fool repeats his folly (26:11).

Though you grind a fool in a mortar with a
    pestle
Along with crushed grain,
Yet his foolishness will not depart from him
    (27:22).

If a wise man contends with a foolish man,
Whether the fool rages or laughs, there is no
    peace (29:9).

The Man of Great Wrath

A man of great wrath will suffer punishment;
For if you deliver him, you will have to do it
    again (19:19).

The Man of Hasty Words

Do you see a man hasty in his words?
There is more hope for a fool than for him
    (29:20).

The Conceited Man

Do you see a man wise in his own eyes?
There is more hope for a fool than for him
    (26:12).

═30═

The Lord Will Reward

Evil pursues sinners,
But to the righteous, good
shall be repaid (13:21).

People usually hope for a recompense of reward for present deeds and future destiny. Solomon frequently reminded his pupils that such
rewards are awarded according to works,
whether good or bad. The award may be given
in this life or in the life to come; God decides.
In similar fashion, good government should
reward citizens according to their deeds, good
or evil. But in any case, one must not avenge
himself but must leave the matter to God and
civil government.

God recompenses righteousness, or the lack of
it: He rewards mercy, integrity, and faithfulness,
among other virtues. He recompenses
unrighteousness such as bloodshed, disrespect,
greedy haste, injustice, oppression, partiality,
perverseness, pride, rebellion, and treachery.
This recompense rightly includes punishment

even for such folly as anger, lack of foresight, and impulsiveness. The guilty must not escape punishment, because punishment deters the evil inclinations of others. God does not condone the unjust punishment of the righteous. The wise work for worthy rewards.

Reward Is According to Works, Good or Evil

The fear of the LORD prolongs days,
But the years of the wicked will be shortened.
The hope of the righteous will be gladness,
But the expectation of the wicked will perish.
The way of the LORD is strength for the upright,
But destruction will come to the workers of
 iniquity (10:27–29).

The wicked man does deceptive work,
But to him who sows righteousness will be a
 sure reward.
As righteousness leads to life,
So he who pursues evil pursues it to his own
 death (11:18–19).

He who diligently seeks good finds favor,
But trouble will come to him who seeks evil
 (11:27).

A man will be satisifed with good by the fruit
 of his mouth,
And the recompense of a man's hands will be
 rendered to him (12:14).

The house of the wicked will be overthrown,

But the tent of the upright will flourish.
The evil will bow before the good,
And the wicked at the gates of the righteous
 (14:11, 19).

In the house of the righteous there is much
 treasure,
But in the revenue of the wicked is trouble
 (15:6).

The fear of the LORD leads to life,
And he who has it will abide in satisfaction;
He will not be visited with evil (19:23).

The righteous God wisely considers the house
 of the wicked,
Overthrowing the wicked for their wickedness
 (21:12).

It is a joy for the just to do justice,
But destruction will come to the workers of
 iniquity (21:15).

He who sows iniquity will reap sorrow,
And the rod of his anger will fail (22:8).

By transgression an evil man is snared,
But the righteous sings and rejoices (29:6).

When the wicked are multiplied, transgression
 increases;
But the righteous will see their fall (29:16).

Reward Is Often in This Life

If the righteous will be recompensed on the
  earth,
How much more the wicked and the sinner
  (11:31).

Reward Is in the Life to Come

The LORD has made all things for Himself,
Yes, even the wicked for the day of doom
  (16:4).

Good Government Rewards
Both Good and Evil

The king's favor is toward a wise servant,
But his wrath is against him who causes shame
  (14:35).

Do Not Avenge Yourself

Do not say, "I will recompense evil";
Wait for the LORD, and He will save you
  (20:22).

Do not say, "I will do to him just as he has
  done to me;
I will render to the man according to his work."
  (24:29).

God Recompenses Righteousness

Mercy

The merciful man does good for his own soul,
But he who is cruel troubles his own flesh
 (11:17).

He who has pity on the poor lends to the LORD,
And He will pay back what he has given
 (19:17).

Deliver those who are drawn toward death,
And hold back those stumbling to the slaughter.
If you say, "Surely we did not know this,"
Does not He who weighs the hearts consider it?
He who keeps your soul, does He not know it?
And will He not render to each man according
 to his deeds? (24:11–12).

If your enemy is hungry, give him bread to eat;
And if he is thirsty, give him water to drink;
For so you will heap coals of fire on his head,
And the LORD will reward you (25:21–22).

Whoever shuts his ears to the cry of the poor
Will also cry himself and not be heard (21:13).

Integrity

The righteous man walks in his integrity;
His children are blessed after him (20:7).

Bread gained by deceit is sweet to a man,
But afterward his mouth will be filled with
 gravel (20:17).

Faithfulness

Whoever keeps the fig tree will eat its fruit;
So he who waits on his master will be honored
   (27:18).

The eyes of the LORD preserve knowledge,
But He overthrows the words of the faithless
   (22:12).

God Recompenses Unrighteousness

Bloodshed

A man burdened with bloodshed will flee into a
   pit;
Let no one help him (28:17).

Disrespect

The eye that mocks his father,
And scorns obedience to his mother,
The ravens of the valley will pick it out,
And the young eagles will eat it (30:17).

Whoever curses his father or his mother,
His lamp will be put out in deep darkness
   (20:20).

Greedy Haste

An inheritance gained hastily at the beginning
Will not be blessed at the end (20:21).

Injustice

Whoever rewards evil for good,
Evil will not depart from his house (17:13).

The violence of the wicked will destroy them,
Because they refuse to do justice (21:7).

Oppression

Do not rob the poor because he is poor,
Nor oppress the afflicted at the gate;
For the LORD will plead their cause,
And plunder the soul of those who plunder
   them (22:22–23).

Partiality

These things also belong to the wise:
It is not good to show partiality in judgment.
He who says to the wicked,
"You are righteous,"
Him the people will curse;
Nations will abhor him.
But those who rebuke the wicked will have
   delight,
And a good blessing will come upon them
   (24:23–25).

Perverseness

Whoever walks blamelessly will be saved,
But he who is perverse in his ways will fall at
   once (28:18).

Pride

The LORD will destroy the house of the proud,
But He will establish the boundary of the
   widow (15:25).

Rebellion

My son, fear the LORD and the king;
Do not associate with those given to change;
For their calamity will rise suddenly,
And who knows the ruin those two can bring?
  (24:21–22).

An evil man seeks only rebellion;
Therefore a cruel messenger will be sent against
  him (17:11).

Treachery

Do not lie in wait, O wicked man,
Against the dwelling of the righteous;
Do not plunder his resting place;
For a righteous man may fall seven times and
  rise again,
But the wicked shall fall by calamity (24:15–16).

Whoever digs a pit will fall into it,
And he who rolls a stone will have it roll back
  on him (26:27).

Whoever causes the upright to go astray in an
  evil way,
He himself will fall into his own pit;
But the blameless will inherit good things
  (28:10).

Recompense Includes Punishment

A false witness will not go unpunished,
And he who speaks lies will not escape (19:5).

Foolishness Will Be Punished

Anger

A man of great wrath will suffer punishment;
For if you deliver him, you will have to do it
    again (19:19).

Lack of Foresight

A prudent man foresees evil and hides himself,
But the simple pass on and are punished.
A prudent man foresees evil and hides himself;
The simple pass on and are punished
    (22:3; 27:12).

Impulsiveness

A faithful man will abound with blessings,
But he who hastens to be rich will not go
    unpunished (28:20).

Punishment Will Not Be Escaped

Everyone who is proud in heart is an
    abomination to the LORD;
Though they join forces, none will go
    unpunished (16:5).

He who mocks the poor reproaches his Maker;
He who is glad at calamity will not go
    unpunished (17:5).

A false witness will not go unpunished,
And he who speaks lies shall perish (19:9).

Punishment Deters Evil

When the scoffer is punished, the simple is
   made wise;
But when the wise is instructed, he receives
   knowledge (21:11).

Unjust Punishment Is Not Good

Also, to punish the righteous is not good,
Nor to strike princes for their uprightness
   (17:26).

=== 31 ===

The Fear of the Lord

Do not be wise in your own eyes;
Fear the LORD and depart from evil.
It will be health to your flesh,
And strength to your bones (3:7–8).

Worship is the willing expression of love, reverence, and devotion for God. Solomon described worship in terms of the fear of the Lord—reverential awe before the all-powerful sovereign creator, and dreadful fear of offending His infinitely holy character. Solomon defined the fear of the Lord by seven characteristics: it is the beginning of wisdom for the sage, the beginning of knowledge for the student, the instruction of wisdom for the scholar, the walk of righteousness for the saint, the fountain of life for the failing, a strong confidence for the fearful, and the hope of the hereafter for the dying.

Worship is of great value to the soul. It leads to life, promises longevity, and may bless with riches and honor. God delights in the sacrifices and prayers of the righteous, but He abhors the

worship of the wicked and regards their rash
vows as a snare. Mere ritual is not acceptable to
God because true worship must be accompanied
by righteousness. Wise men worship in the
spirit of holiness.

Worship Is Wise

My son, if you receive my words,
And treasure my commands within you,
So that you incline your ear to wisdom,
And apply your heart to understanding;
Yes, if you cry out for discernment,
And lift up your voice for understanding,
If you seek her as silver,
And search for her as for hidden treasures;
Then you will understand the fear of the LORD,
And find the knowledge of God (2:1–5).

My son, fear the LORD and the king;
Do not associate with those given to change;
For their calamity will rise suddenly,
And who knows the ruin those two can bring?
    (24:21–22).

The Beginning of Wisdom

"The fear of the LORD is the beginning of
    wisdom,
And the knowledge of the Holy One is
    understanding" (9:10).

The Beginning of Knowledge
The fear of the LORD is the beginning of
    knowledge,
But fools despise wisdom and instruction (1:7).

Instruction of Wisdom
The fear of the LORD is the instruction of
    wisdom,
And before honor is humility (15:33).

Walk of Righteousness
He who walks in his uprightness fears the LORD,
But he who is perverse in his ways despises Him
    (14:2).

"The fear of the LORD is to hate evil;
Pride and arrogance and the evil way and the
    perverse mouth I hate" (8:13).

In mercy and truth atonement is provided for
    iniquity;
And by the fear of the LORD one departs from
    evil (16:6).

Fountain of Life
The fear of the LORD is a fountain of life,
To avoid the snares of death (14:27).

Strong Confidence
In the fear of the LORD there is strong
    confidence,

And His children will have a place of refuge
(14:26).

Hope

Do not let your heart envy sinners,
But in the fear of the LORD continue all day
long;
For surely there is a hereafter,
And your hope will not be cut off (23:17–18).

Worship Is Beneficial

Better is a little with the fear of the LORD,
Than great treasure with trouble (15:16).

It Leads to Life

The fear of the LORD leads to life,
And he who has it will abide in satisfaction;
He will not be visited with evil (19:23).

It Imparts Longevity

The fear of the LORD prolongs days,
But the years of the wicked will be shortened
(10:27).

It Imparts Riches and Honor

By humility and the fear of the LORD
Are riches and honor and life (22:4).

God Delights in Right Worship

The sacrifice of the wicked is an abomination to
the LORD,

But the prayer of the upright is His delight.
The way of the wicked is an abomination to the
    LORD,
But He loves him who follows righteousness
    (15:8–9).

The LORD is far from the wicked,
But He hears the prayer of the righteous (15:29).

God Hates the Worship of the Wicked

The sacrifice of the wicked is an abomination;
How much more when he brings it with wicked
    intent! (21:27).

One who turns away his ear from hearing the
    law,
Even his prayer shall be an abomination (28:9).

Rash Vows Are a Snare

It is a snare for a man to devote rashly
    something as holy,
And afterward to reconsider his vows (20:25).

Righteousness Is Better Than Ritual

To do righteousness and justice
Is more acceptable to the LORD than sacrifice
    (21:3).

NOTES

NOTES

NOTES

NOTES

NOTES

NOTES

NOTES

NOTES

NOTES

NOTES